Knowing Christ Today

Knowing Christ Today

Why We Can Trust Spiritual Knowledge

Dallas Willard

HarperOne
An Imprint of HarperCollinsPublishers

HarperOne

All biblical quotations are taken from the New Revised Standard Version unless otherwise noted.

HarperCollins books may be purchased for educational, business, or sales promotional use. For information please write: Special Markets Department, HarperCollins Publishers, 10 East 53rd Street, New York, NY 10022.

HarperCollins Web site: http://www.harpercollins.com
HarperCollins®, ✦®, and HarperOne™ are trademarks of
HarperCollins Publishers

Designed by Level C

Library of Congress Cataloging-in-Publication Data

Willard, Dallas.
  Knowing Christ today / Dallas Willard.—1st ed.
    p. cm.
  Includes bibliographical references.
  ISBN 978-0-06-088244-0
  1. Knowledge, Theory of (Religion) 2. Christianity—Philosophy.
3. Apologetics. I. Title.
BT50.W473   2009
230—dc22   2009005032

14 15 16 17 RRD (H) 10 9 8 7 6 5 4

Dedicated to the memory of
my sister,
Francis Willard Kohler,
who loved me and cared for me

The *knowledge* of the Holy One is understanding.

PROVERBS 9:10, NASB

I want to *know* Christ and the power of his resurrection and the sharing of his sufferings by being like him in his death, if somehow I might attain the resurrection from the dead.

PAUL THE APOSTLE, PHILIPPIANS 3:10–11

. . . that you may *know* the truth concerning the things about which you have been instructed.

LUKE THE PHYSICIAN, LUKE 1:4

Support your . . . goodness with *knowledge*.

PETER THE APOSTLE, 2 PETER 1:5

THE KINGDOM OF GOD
"In no strange land . . ."

O world invisible, we view thee;
    O world intangible, we touch thee;
O world unknowable, we know thee;
    Inapprehensible, we clutch thee!

Does the fish soar to find the ocean,
    The eagle plunge to find the air—
That we ask of the stars in motion
    If they have rumor of thee there?

Not where the wheeling systems darken,
    And our benumbed conceiving soars!—
The drift of pinions, would we hearken,
    Beats at our own clay-shuttered doors.

The angels keep their ancient places—
    Turn but a stone, and start a wing!
'Tis ye, 'tis your estranged faces
    That miss the many-splendored thing.

But (when so sad thou canst not sadder)
    Cry—and upon thy sore loss
Shall shine the traffic of Jacob's ladder
    Pitched betwixt Heaven and Charing Cross.

Yea, in the night, my Soul, my daughter,
    Cry,—clinging heaven by the hems:
And lo, Christ walking on the water,
    Not of Gennesareth, but Thames!

FRANCIS THOMPSON

Contents

Introduction

THIS BOOK IS about knowledge and about claims to knowledge in relationship to life and Christian faith. It is concerned, more precisely, with the trivialization of faith apart from knowledge and with the disastrous effects of a *repositioning* of faith in Jesus Christ, and of life as his students, *outside* the category of knowledge. This is one result of the novel and politically restricted understanding of knowledge that has captured our social institutions and the popular mind over the last two centuries in the Western world.

Serious and thoughtful Christians today find themselves in a quandary about knowledge, on the one hand, and religious belief and practice, on the other. It is a socially imposed quandary. In the context of modern life and thought, they are urged to treat their central beliefs as something *other* than knowledge—something, in fact, far *short of* knowledge. Those beliefs are to be relegated to the categories of sincere opinion, emotion, blind commitment, or behavior traditional for their social group. And yet they cannot escape the awareness that those beliefs do most certainly come into *conflict* with what is regarded as knowledge in educational and professional circles of public life. This conflict has profound effects upon how they hold and practice religious beliefs and how they present them to others.

Those effects are most clearly seen, on the public stage, in the repositioning of Christian teachers and leaders during the last century. They have been left to preside over the rituals of one or another cultural subgroup that, from the viewpoint of received knowledge, is nothing more than a sociological phenomenon—an "opiate" of certain people—having nothing to do with knowledge of a reality with which all human beings must come to terms. This means that Christian teachers are left in the position of trying to coax and wheedle people into professing things and doing things by some means other than providing them knowledge of reality—hoping, perhaps, for "divine lightning" to strike their souls and bring them around.

The perceived gap between what is counted as knowledge and the offerings of Christian teachers is a reflection of the worldwide acceptance of the science and technology of the Western world, but not of the Christian framework of knowledge that gave rise to it. As Anglican theologian Lesslie Newbigin remarks, however: "No faith can command a man's final and absolute allegiance, that is to say no faith can be a man's real religion, if he knows that it is only true for certain places and certain people. In a world which knows that there is only one physics and one mathematics, religion cannot do less than claim for its affirmations a like universal validity."[1]

A natural outcome of this felt tension between the central things Christians believe and what is accepted as knowledge of reality is the *destabilization* of belief and practice. Belief as *mere* belief—"my personal opinion," as we now ritually say—is already unstable in its own right. As Plato noted long ago, it tends to waver, to come and go, especially when concerned with the more abstract and ultimate issues of life.[2] And that in turn makes character and action based on those beliefs hesitant and variable at best, unsuiting us for steady engagement with the realities (and disengagement from the nonrealities) that we have to deal with. Steadiness in belief and practice then comes to depend upon mere willpower, often taking the form of encrusted close-mindedness or harsh dogmatism. Belief and practice are sustained at great price, if at all. The isolation of faith from knowledge is, accordingly, one major source of the painful difference between what people profess and how they act that is so frequently seen in Christian circles—but, to be accurate, also in humanity at large. This is often thought of as a failure of will or sincerity, but in fact it goes much deeper—it is a matter of whether will and choice are founded on knowledge or the lack of it.

This difficulty is not to be overcome by cultivating or manipulating feeling and emotions, by the practice of ritual or art, or by *trying harder* to believe and act as we think we should. "Just put your hands over your eyes and believe," as some have said. Nor is it overcome by miraculous injections of divine inspiration and upholding from time to time. All of these may have some place. But the problems created by belief *without* knowledge, or belief in *opposition* to knowledge cannot be dealt with in such ways. *Belief cannot reliably govern life and action except in its proper connection with knowledge and with the truth and evidence knowledge involves.*[3]

But, we now are bound to ask, is it *possible* to know the things you believe as a Christian? To what extent? And does it really matter whether you do or not? Doesn't Christian faith automatically relegate you to an intellectual slum? Many—religious or not—deeply feel that it does. Some even think you should be proud of the slum. That is the status history has managed to hang upon faith. The relationship of religion to knowledge has become severely misunderstood and distorted over the last two centuries. In particular, it has become the accepted view that religion *stands free* of knowledge, that it requires only faith or commitment. In some quarters great faith has become equated with a belief or commitment that manages to sustain itself, with great effort, *against* knowledge—or at least with no support from knowledge. Faith is then regarded as essentially a kind of struggle. Some speak of the "lonely person of faith" as an admirable but odd manifestation of heroic willpower.

In fact, such an interpretation of faith is only one part of the larger contemporary picture in which life and action are seen as fundamentally irrational—totally governed by feelings, traditions, force, "willpower," and *blind* commitment. The significance of this picture for our contemporary life as a whole is profound. Like gravity in the physical realm, that picture pervasively influences and guides our thinking and acting—even without any specific awareness of it. In religion its effect upon practice is to restrict the foundation of devotion to will and feelings, with no thought that it is based, wholly or in part, upon knowledge of how things really are. In the social context it leads to mutual incomprehension between disagreeing parties, the inability to seek or find common ground, and suspicion, fear, contempt, and hostility. These are now the persistent undertone of our society and especially of its political discourse, frequently involving religion.

This encompassing outlook on the Christian faith has never been better expressed than by the leading character, Charles Ryder, in Evelyn Waugh's novel *Brideshead Revisited:*

> The view implicit in my education was that the basic narrative of Christianity had long been exposed as a myth, and that opinion was now divided as to whether its ethical teaching was of present value, a division in which the main weight went against it; religion was a hobby which some people professed and others not; at the best it was slightly ornamental, at the worst it was the province of "complexes" and "inhibitions"—catchwords of the decade—and of the intolerance, hypocrisy, and sheer stupidity attributed to it for centuries. No one had ever suggested to me that these quaint observances expressed a coherent philosophic system and intransigent historical claims; nor, had they done so, would I have been much interested.[4]

Within the context of such an outlook, individuals with standing in a particular professional field sometimes feel free, or even obligated, to cloak themselves in the authority of their area of expertise and make grandiose statements such as this by a professor of biological sciences:

> Let me summarize my views on what modern evolutionary biology tells us loud and clear. . . . There are no gods, no purposes, no goal-directed forces of any kind. There is no life after death. When I die, I am absolutely certain that I am going to be dead. That's the end for me. There is no ultimate foundation for ethics, no ultimate meaning to life, and no free will for humans, either.[5]

Logically viewed, this statement is simply laughable. Nowhere within the published, peer-reviewed literature of biology—even *evolutionary* biology—do *any* of the statements of which the professor is "absolutely certain" appear as valid conclusions of sound research. One trembles to think that an expert in the field would not know this or else would feel free to disregard it. Biology as a field of research and knowledge is not even *about* such issues. It simply does not deal with them. They do not fall within the province of its responsibilities. Yet it is very common to hear such declamations about the state of the universe offered up in lectures and writing by specialists in certain areas who have a missionary zeal for their personal causes.

Responsibility to logic and truth has slowly disappeared from our academic and intellectual worlds, over the last century, in response to the pressures of "mass education" and the increasing dominance of "experts." Aristotle, fairly viewed as the originator of the science of logic—though by no means one who brought it to completion—understood that "an educated man should be able to form a fair off-hand judgment as to the goodness or badness of the method used by a professor in his exposition. To be educated is in fact to be able to do this; and even the man of universal education we deem to be such in virtue of his having this ability."[6]

People in the contemporary world rarely understand this any longer and are prepared to accept, or at least not to question, whatever an "expert" or "professor" says, especially if it matches up with what they *want* to be true or with what is fashionable. This is one of the sad effects of what is called "mass education" and especially, at this point, "mass higher education."

Around the middle of the last century C. S. Lewis, through his master devil, Screwtape, spoke of a "time the humans still knew pretty well when a thing was proved and when it was not; and if it was proved they really believed it. They still connected thinking with doing and were prepared to alter their way of life as the result of a chain of reasoning." No more! "What with the weekly press and other such weapons, we have largely altered that," Screwtape continues. He goes on to chide his underdevil, Wormwood, for trying to use *argument* to keep his "patient" from the Enemy's (God's) clutches. "Jargon, not argument, is your best ally in keeping him from the Church. Don't waste time trying to make him think that materialism is *true*! Make him think it is strong or stark or courageous—that it is the philosophy of the future. That's the sort of thing he cares about." (Today, no doubt, we could substitute that it is "scientific" or the result of "research.") Screwtape goes on to warn Wormwood that "by the very act of arguing, you awake the patient's reason; and once it is awake, who can foresee the result?"[7]

Lewis, I think, could hardly have imagined where the tendency toward "slogans," which he notes, would have come by now. Today Christians and non-Christians alike stand within an intellectual atmosphere where politically dominated authority is the primary force at work, and almost no one any longer knows the meaning or application of *Non sequitur,* "It does not follow" (i.e., it is an unwarranted conclusion or assertion). An understanding of ordinary logic is no longer a required part of university degree programs, as was almost universally the case sixty years ago. Now, as a result, our world is full of uneducated people with higher degrees. They have no independent logical judgment and simply conform to what their circle takes to be the "best professional opinion." Thankfully, there are rare exceptions.

The implications of this are ominous and vast for all of us. In what follows I am mainly concerned about the harmful effects of this smothering outlook upon sincere Christians. Make no mistake about it, it is an outlook that undermines the spiritual life of those who would follow Jesus Christ. These people usually get, whether they want it or not, precisely the "education" that Waugh's character mentions and that our professor of biological sciences proclaims as obvious; but they also long to live the life they see in Jesus himself and in his followers at their best. Such an "education" and such a life are inconsistent. They cannot inhabit the same person. *A life of steadfast discipleship to Jesus Christ can be supported only upon assured knowledge of how things are, of the realities in terms of which that life is lived.* As in any arena of real life where knowledge is essential, infallibility is not required, of course, and numerous things to which ordinary Christians (or even lengthy traditions) have subscribed could be erroneous or, so far as their knowledge extends, groundless. Still, a steady life directed, in a communal setting, toward the good and right *can be supported only within a framework of basically sound knowledge and understanding.* This does not fundamentally change when we come to religion. Indeed, there it is more important than ever.

My hope here is to enable intellectually serious people, Christians or not, to understand the *indispensable role of knowledge in faith and life.* I also want to make it clear that *there is a body of uniquely Christian knowledge,* one that is available to all who would appropriately seek it and receive it—again, whether Christians or not. Like all knowledge of any complexity and depth, that body of knowledge does not jump down one's throat, and no one can force it upon another. It has to be welcomed to be possessed. And because, in this case, it is essentially a *knowledge of persons*, it has the special characteristics and makes the special demands upon the knower peculiar to that kind of knowledge. But it is available, and available *as knowledge*, to those of normal human abilities who seek it in ways suited to its subject matter. When understood and accepted as knowledge, it is objectively testable—again, in ways suitable to its subject matter—and it lays a foundation for action and character that is unequaled for human good.

Though my main concern is for the unwarranted burden sincere Christians and Christian teachers find themselves under in the contemporary world of educational thought and practice, knowledge and the will to know, by their very nature, place one in the *common arena of human life*, in the "public square," as is now said. That is one of the most important things about knowledge and the effort to know. It provides a meeting place for all who love and respect their neighbors. It encourages us to listen as well as speak, to learn as well as teach. Knowledge opens up possibilities and imposes responsibilities in the public arena. It is no longer just a matter of "my stuff" against "your stuff." When we step into its arena there is suddenly a "we" and an "ours." Instead of automatic deadlock, there is the possibility of joint inquiry. So, as I write here, I am speaking to every person and responsible to every person.

For most of Western history, the basic claims of the Christian tradition have in fact been regarded by its proponents *as knowledge of reality*, and they were presented as such. You cannot understand the history of the European peoples unless you understand that. Indeed, a similar point is to be made of *all* religions and their cultures. Religion as actually lived, not as some figment of the academic imagination, always claims to involve knowledge of *how things are*. That is of the nature of religion. One cannot seriously imagine the Buddha, for example, presenting his teachings merely as his sentiments, guesses, "personal commitments," or a "leap of faith." Nor did those who heard him and followed him understand him in that way. They understood him as conveying a true picture of profound realities, and as doing so on the basis of knowledge he had gained from his thought and experiences.[8]

The same is true of Moses, Jesus, Muhammad, and teachers from farther east. Contemporary teachers and leaders in religion may not put things that way. But you will notice they also do not have the power and influence of those who founded their religion. If the founders had spoken as they do today, the corresponding religions simply would not be here.

It is one of the curiosities of Western intellectual history that, during the last century or so, those with no serious involvement with practical Christianity—maybe totally ignorant of it or even hostile to it—have been allowed, under the guise of "scholarship" or innovative thought, to define what religion is and to reinterpret Christian teachings in the light of their own biased definitions and purposes. This is now built into our educational system. Then, quite naturally, religion turns out to be something resting upon anything but knowledge, for if it turned out to be a matter of knowledge of reality, then our scholars, as "men and women of science and rationality," would have to accept the knowledge and reality involved or else be counted as irrational themselves. Thus they present religion as an irrational projection or development of some sort—contrary to the inner nature of the religious consciousness itself.[9]

That approach is often combined today with the thought that the basic teachings of Christianity—the existence of a personal God, his intervention and direction in human affairs, the spiritual nature of human beings, the fundamental reliability of the Bible and the central teachings of the church, and so forth—*have been discovered* to be false or without credible evidence. In short, Christianity has been "found out," and it is at best only a set of humanly contrived myths and traditions, if not an outright fraud. Many who have standing as scholarly spokespeople for Christianity promote that view.

Though the task of this book is to deal at length with main points involved in this general, secularist outlook, let us say immediately that the developments of modern thought *have not shown* the substance of Christian teaching to be false or groundless. There have been many discoveries, to be sure, but none producing that result, or even close. Modern discoveries, therefore, have *not* shown that Christianity's central teachings do not or cannot form *a body of knowledge* accessible to capable and responsible inquirers. Certainly the currently prevailing myth of intellectual and academic life is that this *has* been shown. But myth making, as it turns out, is not the sole prerogative of religion. It is also a very active secular and academic pastime—and a human one as well; perhaps it is some kind of human necessity.

But, as we have noted, problems with the relationship between knowledge and Christian teachings and practice are posed not just by those who oppose Christianity or religion, but by those who advocate it. Religious people in the Western world now tend to be uneasy or suspicious about knowledge; they no longer see it as a friend, but, more likely, as an enemy. We begin, therefore, with some highly necessary clarifications of connections between knowledge and life. We hope to show the way in which *knowledge is a friend of faith*, essential to faith and to our relationship with God in the spiritual life.

I should alert readers to the fact that this is not a devotional book and that it will require considerable mental effort to understand. This lies in the nature of the problems to be dealt with. I have tried to ease the pain as much as possible. One result of the displacement of faith from knowledge, which we are dealing with in this book, is that many people now believe you do not need to think deeply and carefully to follow Christ. C. S. Lewis makes a very penetrating comment about this matter:

God has room for people with very little sense, but He wants everyone to use what sense they have. The proper motto is not "Be good, sweet maid, and let who can be clever," but "Be good, sweet maid, and don't forget that this involves being as clever as you can." God is no fonder of intellectual slackers than of any other slackers. If you are thinking of becoming a Christian, I warn you you are embarking on something which is going to take the whole of you, brains and all. . . . One reason why it needs no special education to be a Christian is that Christianity is an education itself.[10]

ONE

Can Faith Ever Be Knowledge?

For it is the God who said, "Let light shine out of darkness," who has shone in our hearts to give the light of the knowledge of the glory of God in the face of Jesus Christ.

PAUL, 2 CORINTHIANS 4:6

A RE THE CENTRAL teachings of the Christian tradition things that can be *known* to be true if appropriately examined? Are they possible subjects of *knowledge*? Are there people who actually do know them to be true? Or are they things you can only *believe* or choose to *commit* yourself to, perhaps only *profess*? And does it really matter one way or the other? If so, why?

Consider just the Apostles' Creed:

I believe in God, the Father Almighty, Maker of heaven and earth, and in Jesus Christ, his only Son, our Lord, who was conceived by the Holy Spirit, born of the Virgin Mary, suffered under Pontius Pilate, was crucified, dead, and buried. He descended into hell. The third day he rose again from the dead. He ascended into heaven, and sits on the right hand of God, the Father Almighty. From thence he shall come to judge the quick and the dead. I believe in the Holy Spirit, the holy Catholic Church, the communion of saints, the forgiveness of sins, the resurrection of the body, and life everlasting.

This creed is widely regarded and used among Christians as an expression of belief or faith—and possibly of mere commitment or profession where genuine belief is lacking but wanted. But can we also *know* that what is expressed in these beliefs is true and real? And does it matter whether we know what they express or not? Wouldn't it be enough to just believe them? That is often suggested. Mere belief as a heroic act—or even as the result of a miracle—might warrant God's favor.

Of course, we can fail to know the articles of the creed—no doubt about that—and many people do. Just as someone might, for lack of appropriate application, fail to know the multiplication tables, the order of succession of American presidents, or the capital cities of the fifty states. If we don't know those things, however, it is because of an omission on our part. We might believe them without knowing them, of course, but we also can come to know them if we make a point of it. With that everyone agrees. Not knowing them says nothing about the possibility or impossibility of knowledge of them, or about the advantages of knowing them instead of only believing them or being totally ignorant of them. Could the same be true of the Apostles' Creed? Could it be true of the other central teachings of the Christian tradition?

These are important questions for how we live our lives. Almost everyone today is prepared to say that those teachings of Christianity *cannot* be things we know and that, in this respect, they are like the teachings of *every* religion. We in the United States live under a social consensus that seems to require such a response. According to it, the teachings of religion are not possible subjects of knowledge. But we must not accept this conclusion without question, for its implications are of profound importance.

They place the teachings of religion at a crushing disadvantage before all that passes for knowledge in our world. They relegate them to practical irrelevance and loosen any grip they might otherwise have on the understanding and direction of life. Is that really justified? Or is it a terrible mistake? The difference between belief and knowledge is huge and affects every area of life. Not having knowledge of the central truths of Christianity is certainly one reason for the great disparity between what Christians profess and how they behave—a well-known and disturbing phenomenon.

KNOWLEDGE, BELIEF, COMMITMENT, AND PROFESSION

We must begin to rethink these matters by reflecting on what knowledge is. What is it to know, to possess knowledge of a certain subject matter? We cannot here plumb this question to its depths, but a working idea, derived from how we actually deal with knowledge in real life, is this: *We have knowledge of something when we are representing it (thinking about it, speaking of it, treating it) as it actually is, on an appropriate basis of thought and experience.* Knowledge involves truth or accuracy of representation, but it must also be truth based upon adequate evidence or insight. The evidence or insight comes in various ways, depending on the nature of the subject matter. But it must be there.

Knowledge in this sense is what we require in service people, professionals, and leaders. We expect them to *know* what they are doing, to be right, but *not* just by guessing or luck. We might occasionally accept luck in an automobile mechanic—far less so in a brain surgeon or a government official—but even then only if it comes in a context of solid knowledge and steady practice based on it. Those professionals must not *count on* luck. You would not take your car to a shop that advertised itself as being lucky in making repairs. Luck cannot be the modus operandi. Knowledge brings truth and correctness under reliable control. That is what we need and want in real life, and what we regularly have. But how does that differ from belief?

Belief, by contrast, has no necessary tie to truth, good method, or evidence. We can believe what is false and often do. Belief may arise from many sources. Children and others "catch" beliefs from those around them. Emotions such as fear, hatred, or love give rise to beliefs. In its basic nature belief is a matter of *tendencies to act.* It has a certain feeling tone to it in some cases, but to believe something involves a readiness to act, in appropriate circumstances, *as if* what is believed were so. Thus belief involves the will in a way that knowledge does not. If I believe I am low on gas, I will have an eye out for a gas station and be ready to turn in and fill up if things seem right. If I believe I have plenty of fuel, on the other hand, my thoughts, feelings, tendencies, and behaviors will be characteristically different. But of course I could be wrong either way and *still* believe. My fuel gauge may have gone crazy, or my friend, who loaned me the car, may have misinformed me about the need for fuel.

Similarly, if I really do believe in God, I will tend to act as if he exists. If I believe that the Bible and the church are unique sources of reliable information about life and well-being, I will tend to honor them and give them careful attention, making them a part of my life. If I believe they are not, I will avoid them or even attack them.

But what about commitment? Is it the same as belief? Not at all. *Commitment,* made so much of today in religion and in life, need not involve belief, much less knowledge. You can commit yourself to something you don't even believe. Commitment is simply a matter of choosing and implementing a course of action. We have that ability. It is part of what humans can do. Sometimes we have to act when we "don't know what to do" or even when we have no belief concerning what would be best. Time and circumstance are passing. A person lost in a forest may have no idea of which direction to take, but commit in action to one particular direction because the person knows or believes he or she must do *something*. Or an investment must be made *now*, for example, or a relationship engaged in. We then commit ourselves to a course of action, because we must do something. Or perhaps, on rare occasion, we wish to be arbitrary, to just have a fling and see what happens. That is how we board a roller coaster.

At an even greater distance from knowledge is *profession*. Sometimes people *profess* to believe things they are not even committed to. They may do this just to fit into a social setting. Throughout history, and in some places still today, professing to believe things they don't believe, or even things they are committed against, has been the only way for people to save their lives or avoid great harm. This was true of Jews and Muslims in Spain at one time and is true for Christians in many parts of our world today. Professing to believe has, sadly, played a large role in the *practice* of religion. It has profoundly stained our understanding of what religion is. Some people seem to profess belief in God "just in case" there is a God. But they neither are committed to nor believe in the idea that God exists.

WHY KNOWLEDGE MATTERS

With these distinctions before us, we can see how important the answer is to the question of whether religious or other teachings are subjects of knowledge. It makes a huge difference in the conduct of life and for human well-being. *Knowledge, but not mere belief or commitment, confers on its possessor an authority or right—even a responsibility—to act, to direct action, to establish and supervise policy, and to teach.* Circumstances will modify this from case to case, but it is in general true. Knowledge also confers upon belief and action a stability and communicability that other sources of action do not. This is because knowledge involves truth: truth secured by experience, method, and evidence that is generally available.

And that explains why we want leaders, professionals, and others we rely upon to *know* what they are doing, not just to believe or feel strongly about it. We trust them on the assumption or the hope that they know their area of expertise, even if we are mistaken about them in a given case. Beliefs, commitments, feelings, traditions, and power do *not* confer on them the same right and authority as knowledge does, even if those things sometimes happen to coincide with a correct outcome. We are still aware that those sources of action might have been wrong and that they lack any basis that ensures their rightness—especially, any basis that can be shared and openly evaluated in fair inquiry by those affected. Clearly, our belief (trust, confidence, faith) in those who guide or help us assumes that they have knowledge. If they lack the knowledge assumed, they are disqualified, even if they remain in a position of service or power.

It is a mistake to think of belief simply as knowledge *manqué*, as something that falls short of knowledge or is deficient knowledge. Belief does not "turn into" knowledge, though we sometimes come to know what we previously only believed. Rather, *belief and knowledge are different kinds of things with different roles in life*. Belief does not necessarily disappear when knowledge comes. Of two people who share a belief, one can also know what they both believe, and the other not. This is typical of teachers and students or of experts and nonexperts in a given area. Certainly we often believe what we do not, and perhaps cannot, know. We would be in a pretty pickle if we could not do that, for knowledge is not always available to guide action when we need it. But it is less widely recognized that *we sometimes do not believe what we know*. For example, most people who enter the lottery know they will not win. They will not win, and they have good evidence that they will not. They may refuse to consider the evidence or to hold it before their mind. Yet they are prepared to *act as if* they might win. In wagering they are irrational and irresponsible. Human life is full of such self-delusions.

And that explains why gambling is morally wrong. It is not a morally admirable practice, but just the opposite. Rational and responsible persons will not do it. (We have a duty to be rational. It is a virtue.) And it also explains why the gambling industry presents itself as "entertainment." It wants to disguise what it really is. When you gamble, according to it, you are just "enjoying yourself" or having a fling. But rational and responsible people are those who strive to base their beliefs and actions upon their knowledge.

We must not overlook this when thinking about the relationship between knowledge and belief, and between knowledge and Christian faith. It is desirable to base our beliefs on knowledge wherever possible. Knowledge stabilizes true belief and makes it more effectual for good as well as more accessible and shareable. We cannot understand this if we are thinking of belief as only a preliminary to knowledge, one that disappears when knowledge arrives. Ideally, knowledge is the basis of belief, and, when it is, it gives the belief a very different bearing upon life. *Knowledge is a basis for belief,* the very best basis, but belief is not a basis for knowledge or even a constituent of it. Thus we come by the idea of mere "head knowledge"—it is knowledge without belief, and perhaps it is mere profession.

RELIGION ALWAYS PRESENTS ITSELF AS BASED ON KNOWLEDGE

The central teachings of the Christian religion, such as those of the Apostles' Creed, were from the beginning presented and accepted as knowledge—knowledge of what is real and what is right.[1] That is why they had the transforming effect they did on a world dead set against them. Indeed, the biblical tradition as a whole presents itself, rightly or wrongly, as one of *knowledge of*

God. Then, within that overarching context of knowledge, there do arise specific occasions of faith and commitment to action extending beyond what is known, but still conditioned upon the knowledge of God. Consider the biblical stories. When, for example, Abraham left his homeland and went out "not knowing" where he was going, he did so *because* of his knowledge of God and of God's constant care in his life. He did not do it wondering whether God existed or was with him. The same was true of his willingness to offer up his son Isaac. The very ground of his actions in faith without specific knowledge was precisely overarching knowledge of his God, who spoke to him and acted in his life.

The same is true of Moses when he went in faith to deliver the Israelites from slavery, and of David when he went into battle against Goliath. Moses, according to the texts, is given conclusive evidence that God is with him—evidence he also can present to others (Exod. 3–4). David actually cites, to those who doubted his ability, the experiences and the knowledge that enabled him to believe he could conquer the giant (1 Sam. 17:34–37). Over and over in the Old Testament the explanation of events in human history is that humans may *know* that Jehovah is the living God.[2] *An act of faith in the biblical tradition is always undertaken in an environment of knowledge and is inseparable from it.*

We can never understand the life of faith seen in scripture and in serious Christian living unless we drop the idea of faith as a "blind leap" and understand that faith is commitment to action, often beyond our natural abilities, *based upon knowledge of God and God's ways.* The romantic talk of "leaping," to which we in the Western world have become accustomed, actually amounts to "leaping" *without* faith—that is, with no genuine belief at all. And that is actually what people have in mind today when they speak of a "leap of faith."

The biblical stories know absolutely nothing of blind "leaps of faith," as that phrase is now understood. Such "leaps" are a pure fantasy imposed upon those stories and upon the religious life by the prejudices and tortured turns of modern thought. The result has been to undermine the *foundations of faith in knowledge* and to leave the teachings of Jesus and his people (along with those of all other religions) hanging in the air, with no right or responsibility to direct human life. That also explains how many people can now say, "All religions are equal." What is meant is that all religions are equally devoid of knowledge and reality or truth. In fact, however, no known religions are the same; they teach and practice radically different things. You only have to look at them to see that. To say they are all the "same" is to disrespect them. It is a way of claiming that none really matter, that their distinctives are of no human significance.

Alvin Plantinga is one of the most highly regarded American philosophers of recent decades. In virtue of his research and publications, no one today has clearer insight into knowledge and belief than he does. He rightly points out that knowledge is an essential element of Christian faith, and he dismisses the common assumption that one can only believe that God exists, but cannot know it. He remarks: "The Bible regularly speaks of *knowledge* in this context—not just rational or well-founded belief. Of course, it is true that the believer has *faith*—faith in God, faith in what He reveals—but this by no means settles the issue. The question is whether he doesn't also *know* that God exists. Indeed, according to the Heidelberg Catechism, knowledge is an essential element of faith, so that one has true faith that *p* only if he knows that *p*."[3]

The language of the New Testament documents is starkly clear on the centrality of knowledge to following Jesus. It even defines or describes *eternal life* as knowledge. Jesus speaks of the eternal kind of life he brings to his people: "And this is eternal life, that they may *know* you, the only true God, and Jesus Christ whom you have sent" (John 17:3; cf. 1 John 1:1–5; 2:3; 4:7–8, 13). We shall have much more to say later on about this knowledge that *is* the eternal kind of life. But for now we only recall the ringing declarations of Paul: "I want to *know* Christ and the power of his resurrection and the sharing of his sufferings" (Phil. 3:10; all emphases in scriptural quotations have been added), and "I *know* the one in whom I have put my trust" (2 Tim. 1:12). Or consider the carefully laid out passage in 2 Peter 1:2–3: "May grace and peace be yours in abundance in the *knowledge* of God and of Jesus our Lord. His divine power has given us everything needed for life and godliness, through the *true knowledge* of him who called us by his own glory and goodness." Shortly afterward we are told to support our "goodness," or virtue, with *knowledge,* as disciples of Jesus (v. 5). Then the admonition is given at the end of this letter to "grow in the grace and *knowledge* of our Lord and Savior Jesus Christ" (3:18). The assumption is that we have knowledge of him and that it can and should continually grow. The book now in your hand is devoted to an examination of this assumption in the context of modern life and thought.

But what is true of Christianity in its inception and history is true of other religions as well. They all present themselves as providing *knowledge* of what is real and what is right. To think otherwise is *to falsify the very nature of religious consciousness and religious life* as well as the claims of the particular religions. If religions only called people to "faith" or commitment (or profession!) as those are now generally understood, they would have no claim whatsoever on the attention of humankind. Instead, they offer—whether they are right about it or not—knowledge of certain profound truths, and they call people to act on the basis of that knowledge.

The "enlightenment" of which Buddhists speak, for example, is offered as knowledge, as passing beyond the false beliefs and passions engulfing the usual human existence and grasping ultimate reality. The Buddha promises *knowledge of how things really are.* Your belief or "faith" is, after all, just a fact of little interest about you, but your *knowledge,* or claims thereto, puts you in a larger context that involves the public. Indeed, one can hardly imagine a religion offering itself on the basis of mere belief or commitment. Why would anyone imagine such a thing? Well, as it turns out, there is a good answer to that question.

THE STRUGGLE FOR THE WESTERN MIND

In the Western world, a great historical struggle between what might be called "traditional" knowledge, represented by the church, and modern knowledge, represented by science, has brought us to where many can only think of religion as *mere* belief or commitment. A significant part of what the traditional "Christian" authority in late medieval and early modern Europe presented as knowledge turned out not to be knowledge at all. Some of it was shown to be false by genuine advances in knowledge, and some of it was found to be based upon unreliable or questionable sources. A pervasive mood of rejection then arose. That mood became an intellectual and academic lifestyle and spread across the social landscape *as an authority in its own right.* It branded *all* traditional and religious "knowledge" as mere illusion or superstition and *all* of the sources of such knowledge as unreliable or even delusory. This mood came, *with no logical justification whatever,* to govern the world of Western thought, and you will see it today in the popular works of anti-Christian and antireligious writers. Over a period of time the status of "knowledge" came to be reserved, as a matter of definition, to the subject matters of mathematics and the "natural" sciences—and, questionably, to that of the "social" or "human" sciences as well.

We cannot tell that whole story here, but it brings us to where, rightly or wrongly, we stand today. Religion, and the Christian tradition in particular—because it was the form of religion that occupied the ground in Europe and North America—lost in the public mind its standing as a body of knowledge about what is real and what is right. It could no longer presume in society at large to direct action, to formulate and supervise policy, and to teach its principles as knowledge of how things really are.

Now, you may think that that is too strongly stated. You may reply that we in the Western world extend to all religions the *right* to believe, speak, act, and teach what they please. But that is not really true, when you carefully examine the facts. And, with little if any exception, it is only a political and legal matter at best. It is not a concession publicly granted because religious teachings are regarded as possibly constituting a body of knowledge. And this is usually agreed to by Christians themselves. Even institutions of higher education that self-identify as Christian do not think of or present themselves as possessing a body of *knowledge* that secular schools do not have. They do not say that the secular schools lack knowledge of reality. They fear public disqualification from the knowledge and research game if they say that.

CHRISTIANS HAVE ACTUALLY ENCOURAGED FAITH WITHOUT KNOWLEDGE

In fact, the Christian churches generally not only *accepted* the elimination of their teachings from the domain of knowledge; they were also complicit in it and even encouraged it. With the burgeoning of modern and entirely secularized knowledge in the 1700s and 1800s, they over time conceded the field of knowledge to a totally secularized "science" and "research." On the theological left, or "liberal" side, this was very largely a defensive move, designed to insulate Christian faith and practice from any possible negative impact of the results of scientific and historical studies. Liberal theology in its earlier periods made the essence of religion out to be a matter of inner experience, including, first, the moral life, which was said not to depend upon matters of historical or other "facts." It later lost the "inner" emphasis entirely and became a version of what is now called "social ethics." The famous gap between fact and value, so dear to the modern mind, did heavy service here. Baruch Spinoza, David Hume, Immanuel Kant, Friedrich Schleiermacher, Gotthold Lessing, and many others lent their weight to divorcing religion and morality from the world of facts and knowledge.[4] In time, religion and morality became merely "political," as they are now for most people. What is political, as now understood, does not require knowledge, but only advocacy. Its only issue is how to "win" for "your side."

The same disconnection of faith from knowledge was achieved on the theological right or "conservative" side of Christian institutions, though upon a different principle. Here knowledge was classed as "works" or as the result of merely human effort. It was opposed to the miraculous work of "grace," which was supposed to produce belief ("faith") *without* human knowledge or even in opposition to it. You are saved by grace through faith, as the apostle Paul famously said, and the faith was a *gift* of God, not a result of human effort, in order that no one would be in position to boast of his or her superiority (Eph. 2:8–9).[5] Knowledge was pushed away as inessential to saving faith, having nothing to do with it. There was no thought that such faith, though still a gift, might actually involve knowledge as an essential part or support, or that knowledge too could be a gift of God without losing its inner character *as* knowledge, possibly even a gift essential to the gift of faith.

So in the recent past Christian leaders and institutions of one stripe or another have abandoned knowledge to the secular mind and even promulgated the idea that if you knew something, you could not have faith in it. That is often said now and in fact has become the usual approach. Never mind that our lives are full of things we both believe *and* know, and that we even believe most things we do believe *because* we know them. We justifiably regard people who in ordinary life believe things they don't know with some caution. And we ordinarily want and expect people to believe things they do know, if at all possible.

The American Quaker theologian Elton Trueblood, some years ago, quoted Kirsopp Lake's definition: "Faith is not belief in spite of evidence, but life in scorn of consequences." Then he adds: "*Faith*, as the plain man knows, *is not belief without proof, but trust without reservations*."[6] This loads a bit too much onto faith, to be honest about it, for faith certainly allows for some reservations. Still, Trueblood was moving in the right direction. Faith has to do with engagement of the will, as we have noted, and not with absence of knowledge—which may come or go in various ways along with engagement of the will.

TOLERANCE REJECTS KNOWLEDGE?

Another line of influence pushing religion and faith out of the range of knowledge has to do with tolerance, or with its opposite, persecution. There has arisen the idea that if you think you *know* what your religion holds to be true, as distinct from merely believing, being committed to, or professing it, you will be *certain*—you will have no doubt about what your religion teaches. That in turn will, supposedly, make a bigot of you; you will be close-minded, dogmatic, arrogant, and high-handed. You will treat "infidels" badly, for they will in your eyes deserve no better. You may then deprive them of their goods, torture them, or even kill them. People who *know* they are right, it is said, are intolerant, and when in power, they are dangerous.

There is some *apparent* historical warrant to this view, but is the problem really knowledge, or is it something else? Possibly the *lack* of appropriate knowledge? And can the solution to the problem of intolerance really lie in denying knowledge, especially with respect to the things that matter most to many human beings, religion and morals? If we can just treat religion and morals as areas in which there is no knowledge, the proposal is, we will have pulled the rug out from under dogmatism, intolerance, and persecution. They will then disappear. Well, one can only say that that is a pretty shallow analysis of the problem of intolerance. Intolerant people often claim "absolute" knowledge, but that does not mean you can get rid of intolerance by disallowing knowledge.[7]

This line of thinking about tolerance and knowledge has become routine in elite cultural circles, however. It is a major part of what lies behind the elevation of tolerance to the level of the few primary virtues recognized today.[8] Several years ago the scientist and intellectual historian Jacob Bronowski produced a television series and a book called *The Ascent of Man*. In the eleventh episode and chapter, he dealt with the great harm done by those who think they know. Supposedly, the harm is done just *because* they think they know. At the end of the episode he strides out into the ash pond at Auschwitz, squats down, and scoops up a handful of mud. "This," he says, "is where people were turned into numbers. Into this pond were flushed the ashes of some four million people. And that was not done by gas. It was done by arrogance. It was done by dogma. It was done by ignorance. When people believe that they have absolute knowledge, with no test in reality, this is how they behave. This is what men do when they aspire to the knowledge of the gods."[9]

There are points here well worth making, but the recommended solution to the problem is to make all "knowledge" tentative, that is, to hold it only if it is open to further testing and critical reflection. That is surely a good idea, for a little knowledge is proverbially a dangerous thing, and knowledge is *never* complete, as the apostle Paul pointed out (1 Cor. 8:2). But Bronowski and others have associated openness and humility about knowledge only with science and scientific knowledge. Other knowledge claims, especially those of religion and morality, are thought by them to have no test in reality and therefore no check on the certainty with which they are held. So claims to knowledge in these other areas must be rejected, they think, and this can be done by simply restricting knowledge to scientific knowledge. That is their solution. Once again, then, religion and Christian beliefs are eliminated from the domain of knowledge.

Faith cannot be "knowledge" or be certified by "knowledge," it is held. But with that it loses the rights, authority, and power over life that are always reserved for knowledge and that are not applicable to mere belief or commitment. No doubt that was, after all, what was wanted by some.

DISOWNING KNOWLEDGE LEADS TO TOLERANCE?

Bronowski certainly regarded himself as expressing moral, though perhaps not religious, knowledge—as not just making a "leap of faith"—when he presses for the elimination of "absolute" knowledge. Certainly he is not expressing a conclusion of any science known to humankind. And it is fair to ask how one can stand against arrogance and intolerance and persecution *except on the basis of* knowledge. Is that not what he is doing—resting his case on what he knows? What else is possible? He certainly did not think he was just expressing his own personal belief or commitment. And is it not true that the brightest examples of people who stand *against* arrogance and intolerance are, for the most part, those who stand on the basis of what they take to be religious and moral knowledge? Wasn't that true of most of those who *did* oppose Hitler and his ash pond? And, just for the record, those who did *not* oppose Hitler usually blamed it, precisely, on *lack* of knowledge: "We did not know this was being done!"

Also, it is not obvious, to say the least, that those who have abandoned religious and moral knowledge are *more* tolerant and less inclined to arrogance and cruelty than those who adhere to it. Human beings routinely assume superiority on many grounds other than possession of knowledge. The sad truth is that people can be just as arrogant from belief, commitment, various associations, or simple egotism as from claimed knowledge. Do we actually find more humility and tolerance, with respect to the things that really matter to them, in those who reject the possibility of religious knowledge than in those who accept religious knowledge?

What are the empirical facts here, and where are the studies that establish them? Let's be "scientific" about *that*.

Tolerance is not indifference, but a generous regard and even provision for those who differ from us on points we deeply care about. To support tolerance—which is not the same as lacking intolerance—more is required than just a lack of certainty concerning differences at issue. We must also care about people. Genuine tolerance itself must be based upon assured knowledge of what is real and what is right. And it always is. It is not a "leap of faith." Tolerance is not the lack of something, but the expression of a positive vision of what is good and right, a vision taken to be solidly grounded in knowledge of how things really are. It has often been considered knowledge that all human beings are equally loved by God, and the call to tolerance was based on that knowledge. It was this type of vision, regarded as knowledge, that led to the abolition of slavery and legal segregation, for example. Such a vision, held as knowledge of how things really are, undergirds the possibility of a neighbor love that comes from the heart and reaches across all human differences.

KNOWLEDGE IS ALWAYS POLITICAL

But it is right—in fact it is knowledgeable—to be concerned about the effects of knowledge and claims to knowledge. They have huge influence, for good or ill, on human life and well-being. It is not just that "knowledge is power," in the sense of power to manipulate physical, social, and psychological processes. It is also *political* power—power to lead and influence people, institutions, and governments. We are right to be wary of those who claim to know. The most horrid of cults and totalitarian systems of government always rest upon claims to have special knowledge, whatever else may be involved. Consider the political ideologies of the twentieth century as well as the more limited but death-dealing cults of the present day.

Knowledge is *always* political, not in its nature or what it is—you can't know by voting or counting votes—but in its *effects*. Of course, if it concerns something utterly trivial, it will not be political, for who then cares? But otherwise it will tend to determine political and legal powers and processes. From our biblical stories, once again, Joseph (Gen. 41:38–49) and Daniel (Dan. 2:46–49) were lifted from the level of slaves to high positions in government simply because they exhibited important knowledge. The struggle of the Christian movement to emerge from Judaism was a struggle over who had knowledge of God and God's will and intentions. The internal conflicts and developments of particular religions are nearly *always* a matter of who has knowledge of essential matters.

That knowledge, and perhaps religious knowledge above all, is political follows from the relationship it has to truth, method, evidence, and life, briefly described above. Because it confers upon the possessor the right and responsibility to act, direct action, set and supervise policy, and teach, it cannot *not* be political. This becomes apparent when we observe the inner circle of advisers of rulers and leaders. Kings, presidents, and executive officers at higher levels gather around themselves advisers who have a reputation for knowledge of affairs. They do this in the hope of leading and directing in terms of knowledge and thereby being successful with their undertakings. In a democratic system, the issue of "Who knows?" becomes a point of constant agitation and strife, because so many people think they *know* and that they should therefore have a voice. Consequently, elected officials and policy makers are constantly having to rally support and defend themselves and their ideas. It is invariably a battle over who *knows* what is going on and what should be done, *not* about who has beliefs or commitments.

This helps us appreciate why, in Western societies and especially in America, there is such a huge drive to *rule* religion and Christian institutions and teachings *out of the domain of knowledge.* By that move religion is stripped of the rights and responsibilities that always accompany knowledge and that would certainly increase its political influence. Secularism—itself always posing *as* knowledge, usually by striving to associate itself with "science" and "research"—justifies itself in determining political and legal processes and outcomes by stepping outside what is regarded as religion.[10] Taking advantage of the historical process briefly outlined above, popular media presents faith as foolishness and certainly as ungrounded in knowledge and reality. This aids the secularist cause. The movie *The Miracle on 34th Street* portrays some Christmastime events involving those who do and those who do not "have faith" in Santa Claus. It describes faith as "believing what you know is not so." In the television series *All in the Family,* the intellectual and moral slob Archie Bunker describes faith as "what you wouldn't believe for your life if it wasn't in the Bible." At the end of a CNN special titled "What Is a Christian,"[11] the voice-over at the exit piously intones: "After all, if you've got truth, it's not really faith at all." That is how faith is automatically perceived today.

Harvard University recently reviewed its general education program. The Task Force on General Education issued its report, which included a "Reason and Faith" requirement. A distinguished Harvard professor, Steven Pinker, criticized the report for inadequately stressing the "ennobling nature of knowledge" of "how the world works." He also thought the report assigned too much importance to "faith." He objected to the very juxtaposition of the words "reason" and "faith," for that "makes it sound like 'faith' and 'reason' are parallel and equivalent ways of knowing, and we have to help students navigate between them. But universities are about reason, pure and simple. Faith—believing something without good reasons to do so—has no place in anything but a religious institution, and our society has no shortage of these."[12] The irony of these statements is glaring. The *identification* of faith with "believing something without good reasons to do so" is a clear indication that the professor needs a good course in what faith is. And his statement that "universities are about reason, pure and simple" makes one wonder where he has been. Has he escaped committee duty? Does he not know how classes are routinely conducted? How academic decisions are routinely reached, how they almost always are dominated by careful consideration of whose *interests* are involved?

THE REAL SIGNIFICANCE OF "SEPARATION OF CHURCH AND STATE"

Thinking of Christian faith as grounded in knowledge, and in some parts to *be* knowledge, is to bring oneself into conflict with some of the most basic assumptions of modern thought and to threaten the foundations of a painfully achieved compromise in social order, one that excludes religion from the domain of knowledge *in order to exclude it in other respects*. In the United States that social order is most visible in the phrase "separation of church and state." There is, of course, a perfectly good and indispensable sense in which that language has application and should be zealously upheld. That is the sense of the First Amendment to the Constitution of the United States. But in general usage today, what it really means is that what religion teaches is not a matter of knowledge of reality. It is, rather, only a matter of what certain human groups have accepted as a part of their historical identity, and what (it is assumed) they are all too glad to force upon other groups and individuals as opportunity offers. If it were seriously imagined that the teachings of Christianity or other religions constituted a vital and irreplaceable knowledge of reality, there would be no more talk of the separation of church and state than there is of the separation of chemistry or economics and state.

Failure to grasp this point helps us understand one reason why so much of Islam seems incomprehensible to Westerners. Practitioners of Islam, and certainly its leaders and teachers, regard its teachings as *knowledge* of what is real and what is right and good. Separation of "church" (Islam) and government would therefore amount, in their minds, to separation of mind and life from reality. Who could be in favor of that? Is there any way to retain a valid separation of church and state, as intended by our founding documents, without treating religion as groundless or even foolish belief and practice? We shall have to return to this question later. It actually poses one of the most difficult problems of contemporary life—one to which Christian knowledge and practice based on it offer a viable solution.

KNOWLEDGE IS NEVER SUFFICIENT

Knowledge *alone* is never enough for human life, of course. That is itself one part of genuine Christian knowledge. And by itself, apart from some adequate moral teaching and discipline (based, of course, upon knowledge), it always "puffs one up"—as the apostle Paul in his profound knowledge of knowledge pointed out (1 Cor. 8:1). Knowledge alone sets us up for a fall. It gives a sense of substance and fulfillment to the self and to society that is an illusion. Under this illusion of substance and sufficiency, it forgets, as that wise man Paul also pointed out, that we only know "in part" (1 Cor. 8:1–3; 13:8–12) and that, as the poet Alexander Pope said, "A little knowledge is a dangerous thing." Christians know that our knowledge is *always* little. We rarely even have any idea of how much it leaves out. (It is this knowledge of knowledge that, along with genuine love of neighbor, enables one to avoid intolerance.) In applying what we know or think we know, the "law of unintended effects" comes into play. When we act with even the best of available knowledge, we really don't know what the consequences will be. We use DDT to get rid of crop pests, for example, and eventually find out that we are also getting rid of brown pelicans and eagles and that the fish we eat are loaded with the poison.

"Scientific knowledge," as that is now understood, will not solve these kinds of practical problems, though much good might occur if such knowledge were better used. Still, in no case can it provide the knowledge and wisdom of how to live or even of how to use the knowledge we have. That is, simply, not what it is about. The best physical, chemical, and other scientific knowledge will not tell us what to do and who to be.[13] You only have to examine it carefully to see that. If some think it might, they would be a great help to a needy world if they would just show how. But we need not wait for them to do that, for we constantly employ genuine knowledge that is not from any of the sciences, and we could not live an hour without it.

In what follows, with the appropriately broadened understanding of "knowledge" provided above, we will apply the Augustinian formula *faith seeking understanding* (Heb. 11:3).[14] Faith, indeed, is not the same thing as knowledge, and it arises in many ways, often independently of knowledge. But it is possible, and a very good thing, to have knowledge of the same things we have faith in. Knowledge strengthens faith, sometimes by allowing us to grasp an item of faith in such a way that it *also* becomes an item of knowledge. Knowledge also can and often has laid a foundation for faith. We do often believe things because we have come to know them, and that is an ideal condition of belief. On the other hand, faith commonly acts as a framework and guide for the development and use of knowledge. Neither is complete without the other.

In what follows we will attend to details and just see how it goes. In J. I. Packer's well-chosen words, "I ask you for the moment to stop your ears to those who tell you there is no road to knowledge about God, and come a little way with me and see."[15]

FOR DISCUSSION

1. Is it true that basic Christian beliefs are not regarded as knowledge today? By non-Christians? By Christians?

2. What is changed, what is lost, when a belief someone has is rejected from the domain of knowledge; that is, when it is discovered that they do not *know* it?

3. Reflecting upon the understanding of knowledge given here, what are some real life situations where failure to know (not just believe) has made a great difference? For example, in a hospital or auto repair shop? In investing? Religion? Politics?

4. What are some of the main differences between belief and knowledge?

5. Christian commitment is a good thing, no doubt, but what should it be based upon? Anything? Or will *nothing* do?

6. Why is it that only knowledge confers the right (authority, responsibility) to act, to direct action, to set and supervise policy, and to teach?

7. Is it true that acts of faith, on the biblical pattern, always presuppose *knowledge* of God?

8. What is your view of "leaps of faith"? Are they in general a good thing? Have you ever made one?

9. Why did religion, during the last century or so, "give away" knowledge to the secular world?

10. Does knowledge make people intolerant? Must one *not* know in order to be tolerant? Is tolerance, as a moral virtue, to be based upon ignorance?

11. Does knowledge *strengthen* belief or faith? Or does it *eliminate* faith?

12. Why has "faith" become something of a joke among the "worldly wise"?

TWO

Exactly How We Perish
for Lack of Knowledge

My people are destroyed for lack of knowledge; because
you have rejected knowledge, I reject you from being a
priest to me. And since you have forgotten the law of your
God, I also will forget your children.

HOSEA 4:6

W E HAVE SEEN how important it is for us to have knowledge, and why mere belief and commitment, though they
have their unique places, cannot be substituted for knowledge,
but actually depend upon it in crucial ways. To say that "the righteous (or just) shall live by faith" does not mean that they live by
blind and irresponsible leaps in total absence, or even in defiance,
of knowledge. It does not mean that the "just" live in a state of
ignorance or stupidity.[1] They do on occasion act in specific ways
beyond what they know, but only within a framework of knowledge that makes such action reasonable. Now we must deepen
these points by discussing *exactly how* the lack of knowledge affects our lives and, in particular, how indispensable *knowledge* of
Jesus Christ is to life in the contemporary world.

KNOWLEDGE: SECURE ACCESS TO REALITY

That people often are seriously injured or even destroyed because they lack knowledge on some specific point is a platitude. Most of us have had some firsthand experience with its truth. Our news media and public life are filled with illustrations day by day. Lack of knowledge is not the only source of great harm to human life, but it is a major one. In general, when we are operating in an unfamiliar context—whether we are aware of it or not—we can badly injure ourselves and others, even fatally. But if we know our environment and our actions well, we stand a good chance of dealing with the realities of the case, avoiding the dangers and capitalizing on the opportunities. That is just common sense.

Hence we rightly place great value on knowledge. To be sure, knowledge is valued for its own sake. It adds substance to our soul and enhances our sense of self. Thus Aristotle points out: "All men by nature desire to know. An indication of this is the delight we take in our senses; for even apart from their usefulness they are loved for themselves; and above all the sense of sight."[2] We like to see, and we strive to do so. We want a house or a room "with a view," and we travel as tourists and treasure photographs, for example. Children at a very early age reply, "I know," when told something of which they were perfectly ignorant. Knowing enlarges them, strengthens them, and they immediately grasp this point.

But quite apart from all that, knowledge is treasured for its usefulness. Thus, for almost every problem of human life, education or research is proposed as the solution. That is an old story, reaching back to Socrates and Plato at least, and it is not an unreasonable one. Socrates was famous for the idea that if we only know the good, we will do it.[3] Probably in some appropriately qualified sense his optimism on this point is correct. Without some qualification, however, it severely underestimates the readiness of human desire and human will to fly in the face of facts, truth, and knowledge and to drag us after them. (That underestimation was the fatal error of classical Greek thought. It could never deal with the presence of evil in public life.) Perhaps such resistance to the good is possible only when the relevant knowledge is inadequately grasped or is rejected *as* knowledge. In any case, we constantly do see individuals suffer because of what they do not know or what they refuse to accept though they do know it. And, given what we have learned about knowledge and life in the previous chapter, we can easily see why their loss comes about. Acting on false or ungrounded beliefs or inadequate information leads to destructive encounters with reality.

People perish for lack of knowledge, because *only knowledge permits assured access to reality;* and reality does not adjust itself to accommodate our false beliefs, errors, or hesitations in action. Life demands a steady hand for good, and only knowledge supplies this. This is as true in the spiritual life as elsewhere.

"WORLDVIEW" AND KNOWLEDGE

There are two different levels at which lack of knowledge takes effect. One is the level of *particular facts or circumstances,* and the other is that of a *general outlook on life and world.* This latter, in its upper reaches, is the level of "worldview." If you don't know about the possibility of a particular investment, for example, you may miss an opportunity that would save your family from hard times or bankruptcy. But if you have no knowledge of how investment works or perhaps do not know that there are such things as investments, then you have a more general problem. In some parts of the world now, AIDS-infected men believe that having sexual intercourse with a virgin, even an infant, will cure them. This is a terrible mistake with horrific consequences. It results in disastrous acts and the destruction of many lives. But it also comes from a broader lack of knowledge of the body, disease, and medicine. It is not just a mistake on one specific point. It shows lack of knowledge with reference to broader and more ultimate issues. How lack of knowledge leads to ruin is clear in such cases, and it is also clear that mistakes at higher levels of generality dictate a wide range of disasters at lower levels.

The words of the ancient Israelite prophet Hosea, quoted at the beginning of the chapter, refer to lack of knowledge at the "worldview" level.[4] And in this case we should notice that the lack of knowledge in question comes from a *rejection* of something *as* knowledge. *We can fail to know because we do not want to know*—because what would be known would require us to believe and act in ways contrary to what we want. It often strikes first-time visitors to large cities, such as New York City, how the residents have taught themselves not to look at the problems surrounding them—for example, the homeless or victims of muggings. Looking makes you responsible. Avoidance is one reason for the lack of knowledge among humanity—knowledge can be and often is rejected.

People do not have to know things they very well could know. As the apostle Paul says of humankind in general: "Though they knew God, they refused to acknowledge him as God, and were not thankful he was God. They let their imaginations run wild, and the light of knowledge went out in their hearts" (Rom. 1:21, paraphrase; cf. Eph. 4:17–19). The rejection and the subsequent loss of knowledge once possessed is a curious and tragic thing to be seen in individual lives and in societies.[5] Whether we have knowledge and are living according to knowledge is a primary indicator of future weal or woe. One of the most curious expressions of human perversity is the saying, "What you don't know can't hurt you." It can ruin your life or even kill you, is all!

Hosea knew this well. In his statement quoted above, he was speaking from the perspective of a tiny people surrounded by gigantic nations. Its origin and survival had been, from the very beginning, due to a supernatural, personal presence that was guiding and protecting it—its God Jehovah. Knowledge of him and his ways was the Israelites' only essential resource. Conforming in practice to that knowledge kept them in harmony with the reality that mattered. But now, the prophet says, they are no longer walking in his ways. They have rejected the laws he gave them as knowledge of reality. Where there is no vision of the reality of God, the Jewish proverb says, people just do whatever they want. They "cast off restraint" (Prov. 29:18). They have no way to rise above their harmful and chaotic impulses. This can be seen by reflection on the hard experiences of Israel, but a candid examination of individuals and societies everywhere reveals it as well. And where people do not *want* to know God, he usually allows them to be without him—at least for a while. When desire conflicts with reality, sooner or later reality wins.

IDOLATRY

The particular "lack of knowledge" Hosea saw destroying his people was, of course, *idolatry*. Idolatry is a mistake about reality, and an error at the "worldview" level. It arises from the crying need of human beings to gain control over their lives. That need is understandable, of course, and it must be met in some way. But idolatry tries to meet the need by *assigning* powers to an object of human imagination and artifice, powers that object does not actually possess. It usually thinks of the object as a living being—monstrous in appearance and nearly always an animal or something animal-like—for it must be capable of *action*. In modern life it is more likely to be some sort of technical device or human arrangement (the government or the "market," perhaps) that we have come to trust. The "idol," then, is more than just the physical object, for it is supposed to have powers that, if humans appropriately serve it, will be used to benefit them. In the end the idol is always intended to be the servant of the idol worshipers and their desires.[6] Thus it is humans themselves who are the universal idol, and that is why Paul calls covetousness idolatry

(Col. 3:5; Eph. 5:5). In coveting I elevate myself to the position of having my way and getting the things I want—regardless of others. But idolatry, of whatever kind, never works out well, because it is, precisely, a flight from reality and, often, from knowledge of reality.

Against this, the tradition of life and thought in which Hosea stood was one that rejected idols and service to idols. It knew that idols do not have any power. They are not "living" and not even conscious. This was a theme constantly hammered home by the Old Testament prophets. Paul was later to say that idols are nothing (1 Cor. 8:4). They can't *do* anything. They are made of stuff that they themselves did not make. Some man shaped them and warms himself and bakes his bread with the leftover wood (Isa. 44:9–20). Jehovah, by contrast, lives, has life, is a *living* God; that is, *he is a conscious, active, powerful being*. He created the physical world, has complete control over it, and has a moral purpose and integrity of his own that cannot be manipulated by human "service" or worship.

Such was the view of the prophetic tradition in Israel. These properties of Jehovah are all tirelessly reiterated in the Old Testament writings, and throughout the Bible they are cited in the opening of prayers as a standard form of address to God. The centrality of the Shema to biblical faith—"Hear, O Israel: The Lord is our God, the Lord alone. You shall love the Lord your God with all your heart, and with all your soul, and with all your might" (Deut. 6:4–5)—lies in the *reality* that it presents as the necessary center of human existence. It is not just an empty ritual or magical incantation, though for many who recite it it may be only that.

It was lack of knowledge of this living reality that Hosea saw destroying his nation. To fail to know the God who was the main source of Israel's life—in the face of all the evidence God provided to Israel—and to then fail, as a natural next step, to organize life around him and his actions was to pursue the path of sure destruction. The prophet saw this destruction unfolding all around him in the collapse of personal and social righteousness that resulted from devotion to the popular idols of the land. And he knew that the ultimate outcome would be the disappearance of the nation of Israel as a corporate, political entity. He was, of course, right. That is exactly what happened. A society is like any living organism; its continued existence depends upon the correct integration of its parts into a whole. That integration *cannot* be present if the society is organized around ignorance and illusion and the moral quality of the citizens falls below a certain level. This is still true of modern nations. The Japan and Germany of the mid-twentieth century are illustrations of nations perishing for lack of knowledge; and that fate can befall any nation, including the United States of America.

What Hosea was confronting was a failure of knowledge at the level of "worldview" and the general disintegration of life that comes from acting on falsehoods at that most fundamental of levels. *Knowledge of Christ*, or lack thereof, is also positioned at that level. That is where it competes for the human soul. It offers reality-based orientation of thought, feeling, and action toward the main factors of human existence, especially toward good and evil. Worldview, simply put, consists of the most general and basic assumptions about what is real and what is good—including assumptions about who we are and what we should do. That may sound terribly abstract to you, but there is in fact nothing more practical than our worldview, for *it determines the orientation of everything else we think and do.*

WORLDVIEW: UNAVOIDABLE AND DANGEROUS

Moreover, worldview is *unavoidable*. Everyone has a worldview. Whenever we act, we act with reference to a "world," a totality of facts, goods, and possibilities. A worldview is, therefore, a *biological* necessity for human beings, because we act, whether consciously or not, with reference to a whole (a "world"). Our "view"

of that whole determines what we shall undertake to deal with or
omit in our actions day by day and hour by hour. It dictates what
we will or will not count on as resources and recognize as dangers. It determines our aims and our means and, eventually, the
quality of our life and the kind of person we will become. Our
worldview is simply our overall orientation in life. You cannot
"opt out" of having a worldview. You can only try to have one
that most accords with reality, including the whole realm of facts
concerning what is *genuinely* good. What is true of individuals in
this respect is also true of social groups and even whole societies
or nations.

One's worldview need not be recognized as such to have its
effects. Much of it lies outside our consciousness in the moment
of action, embedded in our body and in its social environment,
including our history, language, and culture. It radiates throughout our life as background assumptions, in thoughts too deep
for words. But any thoughtful observer can discern the essential
outlines of what it is. What we assume to be real and what we
assume to be valuable will govern our attitudes and our actions.
Period. And usually without thinking. But most people do not
recognize that they have a worldview, and usually it is one that
is borrowed, in bits and pieces, from the social environment in
which we are reared. It may not even be self-consistent.

Jesus gives an illustration of how this works in his story of
the prosperous but foolish farmer in Luke 12:16–21. Because
his crops were very abundant, he said to his soul, "Soul you have
ample goods laid up for many years; relax, eat, drink, and be
merry." But in God's eyes he was a fool. He was not dealing with
reality. He did not have many years. He died that night, according to the story, and his possessions went to someone else. "So it
is," says Jesus, "with those who store up treasures for themselves
but are not rich toward God." The rich farmer's general assumptions about what was real and what was good were disastrously
mistaken.[7]

Thus, because worldview is so influential, it is also dangerous. Worldview is where we *most* need to have knowledge, that is, *secured truth*. Perhaps we cannot have knowledge of our worldview as a whole, and some of its parts will then always consist of mere belief or commitment. But for some parts we can have knowledge if we put forth appropriate efforts, and some parts of *some* worldviews can certainly be known to be false. That itself is also an important bit of knowledge.

THE REALITY QUESTION

The foundational part of a worldview is always *what it considers to be real*. We have just seen how this is the issue with idolatry. We do not need to get lost in metaphysical speculations about reality at this point. In practical terms, reality is what you can rely on. The rich farmer took his possessions to be the central reality of his life, and he illustrates the mistake that also led Jesus to say, "Woe to you who are rich, for you have received *your* consolation" (Luke 6:24). Mistakes about reality lead to brutal encounters with it. Illusion, a mistake about what is real, is what will let you down, what you cannot count on. *Knowledge* of reality tends toward successful and confident interactions with reality. It lays down a reliable path of belief, commitment, and action, even when the realities are grim. When we have knowledge, as we have seen, we are not just guessing, and the anxieties, hesitations, and vacillations that prevail where knowledge is absent no longer control our lives.

The "double-minded" person is someone with a reality problem. The New Testament writer James, brother of Jesus, precisely describes the life of such a person. He says that individual is "unstable in every way" (1:8). *That is what lack of knowledge at the worldview level does to you*. It destabilizes your whole life. Possibly James had in mind the words of Jesus that "no one can serve two masters." The context here is one of asking God for wisdom;

James says the person should just ask, for God "gives to all generously and ungrudgingly" (1:5). But then he says to ask "in faith, never doubting, for the one who doubts is like a wave of the sea, driven and tossed by the wind; for the doubter, double-minded and unstable in every way, must not expect to receive anything from the Lord" (1:6–8).

What is going on here? Is it that God is simply punishing people for having doubts? Is he saying, "Naughty, naughty! I will give you nothing"? That hardly fits with the picture here of God as generous and unreproachful. So there must be something else involved. I suggest that the problem is not on the giving side, but on the receiving side. Because the "double-minded" are, as we say, "on again, off again," *they are not able to receive what they are asking for.* They are unable to *act* upon it. One day or hour they are asking God for wisdom, and the next day or hour they are relying on themselves or others. While they are asking God, they have in the corner of their mind the thought that God isn't going to give them what they need, so they must take care of themselves. They are really relying on two different and incompatible things. And when they are trying to get wisdom on their own, they are thinking about the possibility of God giving it to them. On both sides they are undercut by their inner uncertainty about the reliability of God and God's goodwill toward them. Like the Israelites of Elijah's day, they are "limping with two different opinions" (1 Kings 18:21). It is like trying to walk on two bad legs, needing to favor them both at the same time. It cannot succeed. One must "hold still" to receive the wisdom requested.

WHO "HAS IT MADE"?

The reality question is joined, at the worldview level, with *the question of well-being* or, in biblical terms, "blessedness." In living, we make assumptions about who has the "good life" and about how to get it. This is illustrated by the old "wisdom" of *carpe diem* (Latin, "seize the day"): "Let us eat, drink, and be merry, for tomorrow we die" (Isa. 22:13; 1 Cor. 15:32). The reality assumptions behind such "wisdom" are totally obvious. According to the poet Omar Khayyám:

> Some for the Glories of This World; and some
> Sigh for the Prophet's Paradise to come;
> Ah, take the Cash, and let the Credit go,
> Nor heed the rumble of a distant Drum.

In this view, the good life is the life of *sensual enjoyment of the present moment.* Of course, this comes as part of a total view of the world, which defines your life and character as a whole. If someone were writing a letter of recommendation for you for a position, you definitely would *not* want the writer to ascribe this worldview to you, because it would reveal your overall outlook and personality. And common sense tells us that the person who will "take the cash and let the credit go" is not someone we want to depend on or employ. They have a disastrous worldview that will determine who they are and what they will do.

THE CHARACTER QUESTION

A part of our hesitation in adopting the *carpe diem* view of the good life, or in trusting those who do, is our awareness of its entanglements with another worldview question: *Who is a really good person?* We are deeply concerned about this issue, and we sense that how you answer the reality question and the "blessedness" question cannot be separated from the question of who is *worthy* of admiration, companionship, and support in life—of who is worthy of moral approval. People long to be good, to be worthy, and not just to *be*—from tiny children to the elderly exiting the human scene. There is an education on this point in reading obituaries. They rarely say things like: "She had a great figure, and fine teeth and hair," or "He ate, drank, and was merry." There is a lingering suspicion that you cannot have had a good life if you failed to be a good person, and that to be a good person is a large part of genuine success, or "blessedness."

This third question, of who is a good person, is so vital to our worldview that our answer to it and our success in living out the correct answer affect our health and pervasively tinge all our relations to others. This is the truth behind the—often misguided[8]—concern in America with "self-esteem." If you are convinced that you are not a worthy person, that puts your whole being under constant stress. Your blood pressure and other aspects of your physical health will suffer. Your social relations will be unhealthy, and you may even consume yourself and others with shame and rage. You will probably become depressed or find other ways of turning in on yourself and wounding yourself. Rejection, real or imagined, will be the atmosphere of your daily existence. An awareness of all this, if only marginal, is what relentlessly drives the individual to be good—or at least to be thought so. The tragedy of human life is that we want to be good, but we are prepared to do evil "if necessary." In the human condition some find it "necessary" all too often, because the reality question has been answered wrongly.

THE DEVELOPMENT QUESTION

So the human predicament drives us to a fourth worldview question: *How does one become a genuinely good person?* Our answers to the first three questions will frame our answer to this one and, we hope, provide the means for a satisfactory answer to it. But we have to say that the answers of most people today do not do so. They will have answered one or more of those three previous questions erroneously and will therefore come to a wrong answer to this fourth question or perhaps to no answer at all.

Deep-seated in the American mind, for example, is the disastrous idea that we should pursue happiness. But what is happiness? And what are the realities through which one could achieve it? And how, practically speaking, does one pursue happiness? One might pursue happiness on the *carpe diem* principle. But that can be understood in many ways. It could endorse a sensuality of the present moment or endorse devoting the present moment to improvement of one's character, to serving others, or to serving God. Usually in our times, however, it is some form of sensuality. Our choice between these options will have profound implications for our efforts to become a genuinely good person and to live harmoniously with reality, with how things really are.

We today live in a curious period when almost no one is willing to discuss the question of how one becomes a truly good person. There is now a widespread tendency in American culture to think that everyone is *already* good. This probably arises out of confusion concerning the dignity of the individual or the equality of all people. It seems to many that all you have to do to be *worthy* is just to *be*. They mistake *worth* for *worthiness;* the most unworthy of persons still has worth, value, a certain dignity to be respected. On the other hand, as we shall discuss later, it is now widely thought that there is no objective difference between a good and a bad person, or at least that we do not know what that difference is.[9] So, if that is true, a *method* for becoming a really good person would be presumptuous and pointless.

By contrast, the question of how one becomes a good person was uppermost in the minds of classical and medieval moralists, and their efforts to answer the first three questions were largely treated as preliminaries to answering it. They were acutely aware of the importance of finding an answer to the fourth question, and they thoroughly understood that the well-being of a society depends upon the predominance of genuinely good people. That is one reason why the thinkers of the ancient world turned to Christ in the early centuries of the Christian era. They became convinced that he was the key to human transformation toward goodness.

So, the nature of human life is such that, in its orientation and action, it presupposes more or less complete and more or less consistent answers to these four "worldview" questions. The degree to which the answers presupposed are true and known to be true will be the degree to which they undergird lives and societies where there is harmony with reality and genuine well-being for humans.

JESUS'S ANSWERS TO THE WORLDVIEW QUESTIONS

Now let us consider the answers to the four questions that, speaking simply, Jesus Christ gives. It will help us in doing so if we suppose, for the moment, that he was quite intelligent and knew what he was talking about. That is not unreasonable in the light of his place in world history. His responses to these questions emerge from the ancient learnings of the Jewish nation, and they have been developed through the ages, in various ways, by his followers. But they are fundamentally his, and without him they would never have achieved the status in history that they have. Without him and his answers there would have been no "Western civilization" as we know it.[10] So let us assume that he actually knew what he was talking about and state his answers to the four worldview questions that everyone must come to terms with, implicitly or explicitly.

First: *What is real? What is reality?* The answer Jesus gives to this question is: *God and his kingdom.* That is what you can count on and what you have to come to terms with. In the language of technical philosophy, Jesus was a "Personalist." Trinitarian personality is, for him, the last word on the universe. This ultimate person, God, is the only one who can say without qualification, "I am." He is dependent on nothing but himself, and says "I am *that* I am" (Exod. 3:14, KJV); "My being is based on my being."

The "kingdom" of this ultimate being is *the range of his effective will*. It is, in the simplest possible terms, where what God wants done is done. In theological terminology, the kingdom of God is God *reigning*. Ultimately, everything is in the kingdom of God, though for his purposes he allows some things to be outside his effective will—for a season. And those of us who are not in his kingdom now, not conforming to his will, he invites to come in and has made it possible for us to enter.

Jesus claimed to know this reality on the basis of firsthand experience. He said he had come from the Father and that he was one with the Father (John 16:28; 10:30). The reason many people around him concluded that he really was one with the Father was that his words and his deeds had a power that was not human. For example, they saw him take a few little loaves of bread and some fishes and turn them into a huge banquet, with baskets full of remnants left over. How could he do that? Well, energy converts into mass, we now know, and if you know how to do it and have the energy available, you can turn a little matter into a lot of it. You can make anything you want—even turning water into wine, or calming a storm at sea, or returning the dead to life. This certainly seems to be like God, who in the first place created all of nature by his word. The kingdom of God extends to all of nature. It is God's realm. I think one reason we love nature so much is the sense it conveys of a greater world, of a spiritual depth. But we need to get this right, and nature alone will not help us.

If, at the invitation of Jesus, we place ourselves by belief and commitment under the kingdom of God, then we will be under its care and can come to know its reality. No doubt we would not do that if left to ourselves, but we are not left to ourselves. God is actively seeking those who would worship him "in spirit and truth" (John 4:23).

So that, actually, answers the second question: *Who is well-off, blessed?* And the answer of Jesus is: *Anyone who is alive in the kingdom of God*, that is, anyone who is interactively engaged with

God and with the various dynamic dimensions of his reigning. Such engagement with God is *an eternal living, an eternal life.* Eternal living is, as Jesus said, "that they may know you, the only true God, and Jesus Christ whom you have sent" (John 17:3). But "knowledge" as the biblical tradition speaks of it is always *interactive relationship.* I know that I live in the San Fernando Valley of southern California. My knowledge of the San Fernando Valley is not a set of established truths, though it involves that. It is a living relationship that both mirrors and supports my life. What I *know* of that area, what is implicit in my life, is more than could ever be expressed in language, and there is no need for such expression. It is a sense of place, and place is where one *lives.*

It is, no doubt, a crude comparison to living in the San Fernando Valley, but eternal living is a sense of place, of environment, where God is. In that place, one has no legitimate grounds for worry. Jesus is famous for saying just that. You can abandon yourself to God, who is present. "Let go and let God" is an old and wise saying—unfortunately more widely said than practiced. Daniel's three friends, facing death in a "fiery furnace," were commanded to bow to the image set up by King Nebuchadnezzar. Their response to the king was that they did not even need to think about it (Dan. 3:16–18). Their God would or would not deliver them, but in either case all was well. They would not bow.

Jesus announced in the Beatitudes that even the most deprived and insignificant people on earth could be blessed by living in the kingdom: the poor, those who were grief-stricken, those without reputation or standing (the meek), and so forth. About them he said, "Blessed are they, for theirs is the kingdom of God" (Matt. 5:3–10; Luke 6:20–23). The blessedness was not in their condition of being poor, mournful, or disrespected. They were blessed because they could enter the kingdom, and to be in the kingdom means to be blessed *no matter what else happens.* They can rest in that. Their future in God is secured, and their present condition redeemed. Forever. No matter what.

So, in the worldview of Jesus, being well-off, having the "good life," no longer gets in the way of *being a really good person*. The conflict moralists have for centuries striven in vain to reconcile is reconciled for those living in the kingdom of God. I don't have to surrender my integrity to secure myself and what is good for me. A really good person, as Jesus teaches, is *anyone who is pervaded with love:* love for the God who "first loved us" and who in his Son taught us what love is (1 John 4:9–11). And then out of the abundance of such a kingdom life, we bring love to all with whom we have meaningful contact, our "neighbors." The richness of the Shema life (Deut. 6:4–5) naturally flows into the human scene.

Love means will-to-good, willing the benefit of what or who is loved. We may say we love chocolate cake, but we don't. Rather, we want to eat it. That is *desire,* not love. In our culture we have a great problem distinguishing between love and desire, but it is essential that we do so. New Testament Greek has several words for "love." Two are *eros* (from which we get "erotic") and *agape*. *Agape* love, perhaps the greatest contribution of Christ to human civilization, *wills the good of whatever it is directed upon.* It does not wish to consume it. The teaching about love that still permeates Western civilization in its better moments understands that. The highest call on moral beings is to love. Long before the coming of Christ, this was obscurely understood. Socrates remarked, according to Plato, that "The good do their neighbors good and the bad do them evil."[11] But the Greeks, for all their brilliance, could never solve the next problem in line, which was how one becomes a really good person in the sense just explained. How does Jesus answer this fourth worldview question?

How do you *become a really good person*? You *place your confidence in Jesus Christ* and *become his student or apprentice in kingdom living*. That amounts to progressively entering into the *abundance* of life he brings to us. You learn from him how to live in the kingdom of God as he himself did. There is much to learn after you enter. To go through the door is not necessarily to live in the house.

Our confidence that Jesus is "the One" leads us to go constantly to school with him, taking our whole life with us, and it is in so doing that love comes to pervade our life to such an extent that we are unmistakably *his* students. He said, "By this everyone will know that you are my disciples, if you have love for one another" (John 13:35). He can impose this challenge upon himself as teacher because he knows no one else can produce the human transformation he has in mind.

As Jesus's disciple, I am learning from him how to lead my life as he would lead my life if he were I. You are learning from Jesus how to lead your life as he would lead your life if he were you. Yes, the very life you have. Women needn't worry about being excluded from that statement. For specific reasons built into his mission, no doubt, he needed to be male. But apart from some localized circumstances there isn't a person on this earth Jesus couldn't have been. He came in a lowly form and led a lowly life (Phil. 2:5–11). He relinquished supreme power. He learned to live in the kingdom of God as an ordinary human being. God was also in ordinary human life. "Incarnation" does not concern just the events of his conception and birth. It was the taking on of "flesh" in *all* its human meaning. He could live in your circumstances now. He could be you and still live in the kingdom of God. You can be his apprentice no matter who and where you are. It is as his personal friends, living interactively with him, that we *know* the truth and have the freedom—the power over evil—that comes with such knowledge (John 8:31–32).

So we have these four questions:

What is reality?

Who is well-off or blessed?

Who is a truly good person?

How does one become a truly good person?

These are questions that everyone who would be a teacher of humanity must answer, or at least give a reason why they cannot be answered. That is because all human beings *will* answer them, to their bane or blessing. They will answer them by how they live in their world, if in no other way. The answers are implicit in their actions and character. The questions will initially be answered, rightly or wrongly, by the authorities or customs in which they come of age. That is where each one of us must start. But Jesus and his followers have provided answers for billions of people, answers that meet the tests of life and rise above the impositions of our origin and social setting. Presently we are in a time when his right and authority to answer them are radically questioned. Does he know the truth, and can he enable us to know the truth about these fundamental issues of life?

That is a fair question. Really, an essential and unavoidable question. Only if we ask it and answer it by knowing him and knowing what he says to be true can we move beyond mere belief or commitment or profession. Only so can we place, with him, a firm hand on the progress of life toward what is good supported by what is real.

A FIFTH QUESTION

In the modern period in which we live, a fifth question has pushed its way to the forefront of human endeavor: *How do we know which answers to the four questions are true?* Its urgency for modern life and for contemporary issues is the result of the historical and—frankly—the political struggle between the traditional sources of guidance for life in the Western world, on the one hand, and sources derived from what may loosely be called "science" or "research," on the other.

In current open societies, such as in America, there is a constant struggle over *who has knowledge* concerning the burning issues of private and public life. Religion (or "tradition") and science (or "research") are constantly invoked on one side or the other, usually in the midst of blinding confusions and contempts. Like the people in Elijah's day, as we noted, we limp around on incompatible allegiances. Our social and political institutions are "double-minded." "In God we trust" and "under God" become points of bitter contention among our citizens. What we learn in the classroom and what we hear in most churches and in discussions of public policy simply do not fit together, if they have any connection at all. It is not just an issue of "evolution" versus "creation," as is often thought. Those are actually surface matters. The underlying issue is the question of *how or whether we know* things of various kinds, especially at the worldview levels that govern all the lesser points of belief and practice. If there is no knowledge at those levels, humanity is permanently adrift and at the mercy of force and chance. Modernity has, after centuries of struggle, found no credible answers to the basic questions of life.[12] As it turns out, the universities, our primary institutions of research, simply have no intellectually responsible responses to those questions. That is a fact anyone can verify.

INSTITUTIONS OF HIGHER EDUCATION

Our institutions of higher education, our colleges and universities, stand as the authoritative institutions of knowledge in our society today, following the withdrawal of the church from that position. They are the places we go to learn what is taught as knowledge in our world. They not only stand as the repository of legitimate knowledge, but they presume to determine *what shall count as knowledge* and what *methods* are acceptable as sources of knowledge today. That is why their greatest boast today is of *research*. And the test of "good" research is not truth or knowledge achieved—these are standardly held in contempt—but acceptable *method*, as judged by established traditions of research and by those currently regarded as pacesetters in a particular field.

Accepted method for knowledge is defined by specializations. The result is that the accepted institutions of knowledge today have nothing to say—and certainly no *knowledge* to offer—with reference to the primary questions of life, including the fifth question about knowledge itself, for which there is no corresponding specialization. That is why, in our colleges and universities, there is no "department" of reality, or of the good life, or of the good person and how to become one. You have only to say this to recognize that it is so. There is no intellectually responsible teaching on these matters or upon the nature and limits of knowledge and research itself.

As a matter of fact, however, the worldview questions *are* dealt with behind the back, both by individuals (recall our professor of biological sciences) and by policies and practices. "Answers" to those questions *are* communicated—surreptitiously and implicitly for the most part. Human life being what it is, that is unavoidable, and it is living persons, full of opinions and emotions, who inhabit the events and process of higher education. The universities, whether willingly or not, have inherited the worldview questions from their past because of the role they have assumed in life. They have rejected (as knowledge) the answers from the Christian past of the colleges and universities, but have been unable to develop cognitively defensible answers of their own. This is very largely because, in their effort to be in control of knowledge, *they have redefined knowledge,* through "specialization" and "professionalization," *in such a way that it cannot deal with those questions.* So real life—which must assume answers—is, as a matter of fact, abandoned by our "knowledge institutions" to feeling, force, politics, and "traditions." Ragtag, incoherent "answers" float here and there, with no responsible clarification and critique.[13] That is where our society stands today.

This is not exactly a secret in the broader circles of the intellectual world, and there is some recognition in narrower academic contexts that it is an unwarranted and dangerous position for humanity to be in. Daniel Yankelovich, one of the most respected interpreters of public institutions today, has pointed to the widespread public support for *ways of knowing other* than those now acknowledged within the present academic and professional culture. He notes, "The public believes that science does not have, and cannot have, all the answers, and that other ways of knowing are also legitimate and important." Hence the broad-ranging attention to "Postmodernism." Moreover, there is a "growing suspicion that the nation has lost its way and must now rediscover the path of truth. For all its power and cogency, there is little that science and conventional academic knowledge can do to light this path. . . . Higher education may have to do a great deal more in coming decades to recognize, respect, codify, and clarify the strengths and limitations of nonscientific ways of knowing vis-à-vis scientific knowledge."[14] But how might we make a start in this direction?

HELPFUL LESSONS FROM HISTORY?

Historically, three presumed sources of knowledge have dominated human life in turn, and they have been set in opposition to one another because of the political dynamics into which they have fallen. (1) *Authority* based on historical or social position (mainly in church and government) has mostly dominated human life and is still dominant today in many parts of the world—often where it is least suspected. In European history, the power to know by (2) *thinking*, by *reason* (by René Descartes and others), came to dominance in "intellectual" circles in response to the failures and breakdown of the old systems of authority. The excessive claims of reason led to revolt against it and to the emergence of (3) *experience* as the preferred source of knowledge (the empiricism of John Locke and David Hume, later to become naturalism).

"Science," as now generally understood, actually combines appeals to all three sources, but in undigested and incoherent ways that permit it to be manipulated in the public arena, where policy issues are in question, for numerous unscientific and political purposes. Indeed, nothing would be more helpful in the midst of today's confusions than a thorough understanding of the nature and limitations of "science" itself. But the sciences themselves cannot provide such an understanding, because each one is limited to its peculiar subject matter (which certainly is not "science"), and so the necessary work cannot be done in any way that is "scientific" under current understandings.[15] That reveals the impasse of modern life. Science is the presumed authority on knowledge, but it cannot provide scientific knowledge *of science*.

Bright and well-meaning people often make claims for science that are far from logically warranted. Such is the cultural prestige of science. Owen Flanagan, a distinguished professor, describes himself as "a scientifically minded" person, and we shall take his word for it. He remarks: "The strife between Israelis and Palestinians is another example that involves mutual hatred and suspicion, in part, because of seemingly irresolvable theological interpretations over the fate of Jerusalem." He concedes that "science, of course, has nothing to say about whom God intended to reside in Jerusalem." On this he is surely right. And he might have stopped there—but he just couldn't. "But if pressed for an opinion," he goes on, "I think most scientists would say it is absurd to think that anyone knows what God intended for any piece of earth."[16]

But if science has nothing to say about God's intentions, why should anyone care about what "most scientists" think about them, any more than they care about what most accountants or truck drivers think about them? Have "most scientists" seriously examined the question? As Flanagan concedes, they could not do so within their area of their special competence. So he is just expressing a prejudice, albeit one of a "scientifically minded" person. No science is omnicompetent, nor, very likely, is any chance "scientifically minded" person.[17] But given the present confusions in the world of intellect, this seems to be a point easily missed. Actually, what we see here are the influences of an unsupported worldview.

IS THERE A WAY FORWARD?

We need to realize that the three presumed sources of knowledge—authority, reason, and experience—are not inherently opposed, but are well-suited to supplement each other in the course of real life.[18] Let us return, briefly, to the practical understanding of knowledge that was stated in the previous chapter. We said that *we have knowledge of something when we are representing it (thinking about it, speaking of it, treating it) as it actually is, on an appropriate basis of thought and experience.* Two things should be especially noted about this statement.

First, the "appropriate basis of thought and experience" is open-ended. What it amounts to in given cases is often very clear and depends on the nature of the particular case—the particular kind of subject matter involved. In practical life we rightly have little hesitation, however. Accordingly *authority*, properly applied, is not excluded by this statement as a source of knowledge. Most of the learning we do and much of the knowledge we have is, quite properly, based upon "good authority." Moreover, *experience* is not limited to *sense* experience or to perception of the physical world. And thought (*reason*) is not confined to particular forms and techniques, such as mathematics, but refers to the consciously logical exploration of all kinds of things and their relationships. One must accept the fact that there is no such thing as *the* method of knowledge. Still, we do know many things of many different kinds.

Second, and closely related to the first point, when we do know, we often do not know whether or not we know. It is important to understand that there is nothing wrong with this. In fact, it is probably a good thing. The *subject matter* of knowledge, that which in the given case we know, is *not* the knowledge we might have of *that* subject matter. (The subject matter of geology is the earth, not knowledge of the earth.) Whether we can also know that we are actually *knowing* in a given case, as distinguished from merely representing or believing something, may or may not be possible. Sometimes it is. But it is not required, in order to know, that we *know that* we know. And in most cases of knowledge that issue does not even come up. It does come up in some contexts where personal qualifications or positions of power are at issue, and of course that is often very important. (We may need to know whether certain people have knowledge in a certain respect.) But it has no bearing upon whether those in question actually do know.

The concrete progression toward knowledge, in real life, is always rather messy. Various aspects from the three traditional sources of knowledge are usually—probably always—involved. The attempt to avoid or simplify this "messiness" is one of the things that has driven some people to try to restrict knowledge to a very narrow range. But the result of that, when pushed, always leads to *an elimination of most of the clear cases of knowledge from the domain of knowledge.* (Thus arises the pervasive but utterly insincere "skepticism" of the academy and the classroom.) Usually those restrictions on knowledge themselves do not then qualify as knowledge and can be "politically" enforced only by pressure and power. This is very much the story of "epistemology" or the "theory of knowledge" in Western thought since the collapse of traditional authority.[19]

THREE OPERATIONAL WORLDVIEWS

There are at present three general stories, or worldviews, in serious competition for the hearts and minds of men and women in our world. They function powerfully as background authorities.

They hover over the worldview confusions that prevail in most discussions today. We must keep their influences in mind as we approach the possibilities and actualities of knowing Christ in the modern world.

One is the familiar *theistic story* that has formed Western civilization. This consists of Christianity's four answers of Jesus and his tradition to the four worldview questions. The second is the *nirvana story*, most familiar today through current presentations of the teachings of Buddhism and through many of the popular arts along with "New Age" presentations of various kinds. The third is the *naturalist story*, which often tries to present itself as the findings of science, though it is anything but that. This third one is often called the *secularist story*, which now attempts to dominate our main social and political institutions.[20]

Other tendencies of our day have some claim on attention. Agnosticism and paganism are presences in our intellectual, artistic, and spiritual life today. But they are not really strong contenders for the direction of life. The nirvana story itself is more of a presence than neopaganism currently, but for most people it is at best something to dabble in for a bit of innocuous "spirituality" than it is something seriously to give one's life to. So in what follows we will mainly concentrate on elements of the naturalist story and how they affect the theistic story of Jesus. They are the two main factors in the shambles of worldviews in which we stand today.

FOR DISCUSSION

1. Why are people destroyed for lack of knowledge, even in "ordinary" life? What is it that makes knowledge so important for life?

2. Does everyone have a "worldview," whether they know it or not? Are religions "ready-made" worldviews?

3. Relate idolatry to worldview. How did idolatry destroy the ancient nation of Israel? Japan and Germany in the mid-twentieth century? Could it destroy us?

4. Look over the four great worldview questions. Is anything omitted concerning one's most basic orientation in life?

5. How does the "reality" question show up in day-to-day life? In yours? In the organized world around you?

6. What is most commonly assumed to be the "good life" today? Who is thought to "have it made"?

7. When was the last time you had a thoughtful and thorough discussion with someone about what kind of human being qualifies as a really good person? Ever?

8. What does the "world" now say about how you *become* a really good person?

9. Compare Jesus's answers to the four questions to the ones you might hear or see on the street, on the golf course, in the office, or in movies and advertisements.

10. How does the fifth question—*How do you know the truth of answers to the four questions?*—come to the fore in the modern struggle over the authority and right to give answers to the four questions?

11. What is the authority of "research" in our world today? How has the prominence assigned to "research" by today's social system resulted in there being no accredited answers to the four main questions?

THREE

How Moral Knowledge Disappeared

Lord, to whom can we go? You have words of eternal life.

JOHN, 6:68

K NOWLEDGE OF CHRIST in the modern world mainly came through the massive system of moral values, practices, and understandings that he bequeathed to human history through his teachings and his people. This moral heritage took the form not only of precepts and principles, but of images and stories elaborated in art, philosophical thought, and social and governmental institutions as well as in familiar bits of common language and wise sayings.

His answers to the worldview questions of who is well-off, who is a good person, and how to become a good person were of unequaled power. They have been the socially and institutionally dominant ones in the Western world. They compare favorably, at the very least, to serious and systematic answers to those questions from other sources through the ages. They have stood up well under the most intensive theoretical scrutiny, but they have done even better as a guide to living admirably—even heroically—in the circumstances of ordinary life for ordinary people.

The framework of vices and virtues articulated in working out and applying his principles has no serious rivals as a guide to practical moral understanding. His statement, "The truth shall make you free," primarily a reference to *moral* truth, appears on more university walls than any other statement—though most faculty and students today have no idea of what it means, where it came from, or why it is there.

Christ's system of moral understanding and direction remained as a treasured store of knowledge about the good and the right, to guide us in being and doing, far up into the twentieth century. It was assumed and represented *as* knowledge by social and governmental institutions until well into the middle of that century, though by then it had been under attack by a small group of "advanced" thinkers for some time. It may have been dismissed, but to the present day no plausible alternative to it as a basis of individual and social existence has emerged, nothing that even comes close. Today we are, as a culture, in a condition of simple moral drift. One of the most highly regarded European thinkers of the our day, Jürgen Habermas, recently made the following statement:

> Christianity has functioned for the normative self-understanding of modernity as more than a mere precursor or a catalyst. Egalitarian universalism, from which sprang the ideas of freedom and social solidarity, of an autonomous conduct of life and emancipation, of the individual morality of conscience, human rights, and democracy, is the direct heir to the Judaic ethic of justice and the Christian ethic of love. This legacy, substantially unchanged, has been the object of continual critical appropriation and reinterpretation. To this day, there is no alternative to it. And in the light of the current challenges of a postnational constellation, we continue to draw on the substance of this heritage. Everything else is just idle postmodern talk.[1]

What is said here about the basically "Christian" nature of Western countries was universally recognized and routinely stated a century ago and is certainly still true. Habermas is correct. But that nature has been thrust aside as inconvenient in the disengagement of the academy from the church that has been going on since then. That disengagement has had as a necessary part the obscuring and distancing of the reality of Jesus the person and his radical words and life, which brought him and his "kingdom of God" into the flow of world history.

If you really want to know Christ now, you have somehow to set aside the cloud of images and impressions that rule the popular as well as the academic mind, Christian and non-Christian alike. You must try to think of him as an actual human being in a peculiar human context who actually has had the real historical effects he did, up to the present. You have to take him out of the category of religious artifacts and holy holograms that dominate presentations of him in the modern world and see him as a man among men, who moved human history as none other. You must *not* begin with all of the religious paraphernalia that has gathered around him or with the idea that his greatness *must* be an illusion generated by an overlay from superstitious and ambitious people—mainly that "shyster" Paul—who wanted to achieve power for their own purposes.

Just look at his teaching and his influence for what it has been through the ages—there is really no secret about that—and be clear-minded and fair in your estimate of what kind of person could have brought such teachings and influence upon human life. As for those current Christian scholars who want to cut him down to human size or find him inaccessible, just ask this question. If what he was and said is what *they* say he was—a "gentle cynic," as some have called him, or just an ordinary human being who got caught up in the myth-making of followers who imposed upon him unreal layers of divinity and miracles—and said, would there have been a Christian church and a Christian world order at all?

Would anyone even be interested in what those scholars now have to say about him? The answer will, for most, be quite obvious. Nor would there have been the system of moral understanding that remained in the Western world as a treasured store of knowledge to guide being and doing well into the twentieth century.

THE CONTEMPORARY
REINTERPRETATION OF MORALITY

Most people today realize, however, that a drastic change has occurred in the area of morality, without any special regard to its Christian past. It isn't just that "times" have changed and that to be thought of as good (bad) or right (wrong) has shifted in some respects. Rather, goodness and rightness themselves have changed. Being good and being right are no longer what they used to be in the public mind. They were long thought of as something to be revered and honored and accordingly sought, even by those who did not conform to them. They were regarded as something of which responsible people had *knowledge*. To not *know* the difference between right and wrong, good and bad, was to be incompetent. That knowledge was something of great worth in itself—indeed, something worth living for and something that gave a profound meaning to life. It had a high standing in life and made a rigorous claim, regardless of what anyone might think about it, or whether they thought of it at all. Somewhat like the case with physical law (gravity, microbes, etc.), you could ignore goodness and rightness or be ignorant of them, *but only at your great peril*. They were inevitabilities you had to come to terms with. It was not optional. *This* is what has now changed—not just which things are good or bad, right or wrong, but the very *status* of good and right *themselves* and of the difference it makes whether you are good or right or their opposites.

The results of this radical shift with respect to the status of morality in life are abundantly seen in individual choices and lives and in the language that can and cannot be used in conversation, in public speaking and media, and in the popular "arts." The shift is glaring in the way action is now presumed to have no connection with character and worthiness, and in how people aggressively assert that they are good persons even though they have done what is wrong. But the most substantive manifestation of this shift in status—most revealing of its impact upon life— is the fact that social and governmental policy decisions can no longer be reached, justified, and sustained on the basis of publicly recognized moral values and principles or rules.

FROM MORALITY TO LAW

What is permissible and what is done, much less what is required in social and governmental institutions and policies, are no longer to be decided by reference to what is morally good, admissible, or right, but ultimately in the United States by reference to the Constitution and the U.S. Supreme Court. What they are taken to say is mediated to the street level by the court system, the police, and the political process—often now just by lawyers—with no further essential reference to what is morally right. Winning within the legal and political context is the only way things get settled and sustained to any significant degree, not by determination of what is morally good and right. Such determination is just *not there.*

This is a general description, of course, and you will, here and there, find exceptions where distinctively moral values are invoked in a piece of proposed legislation, a law, a judge's decision, or in a policy or action of a nongovernmental organization. But if the moral values involved are then challenged, whether "at law" or in a public arena, they as a rule cannot be successfully defended, or, if they are, it will be only a "political" triumph. The current understanding of morality will permit nothing else.[2] Meanwhile, at the individual level and in entertainment and art, moral vulgarization proceeds apace without moral shame or opprobrium or any effectual restraint other than the political or economic.

IS THIS MORAL PROGRESS?

This change in the view of morality is widely known and even widely accepted, but the underlying causes are not generally identified or understood. For those who *agree* with the changed attitude toward moral values, the cause of the change is simply the *progress* of social "enlightenment." For them it is a matter of "moral" goodness and rightness coming to be seen for what they really are: mere "constructions" by individual or social/historical will. Long respected moral values are, in this view, simply the expression of some group's triumphant desires. And since they are constructions of the will (however that is to be understood), they can be reconstructed by will.

Even what the U.S. Constitution says, in this now dominant view, is not something that is somehow grounded in the nature of things apart from human desires and decisions or in the meanings attached to its words by those who wrote it or by the age in which they lived. What it says is what it can be *made* to say through processes and by persons who, for whatever reasons, simply have the status and credibility—in short, the power—to make it do so and to carry it off.[3] Thus the ultimate point of reference to determine what shall be done in the social scene today is human desire and will—managed to their own ends by those who have the power to do so—not what is good and right apart from what human beings desire. The determination of what shall be done in society is not now a moral issue at all, but strictly a legal and political one. This *triumph of desire over good at the public level* is the most striking and portentous outcome of the changed attitude toward morality that characterizes North American life at present.

NOT REASONS BUT CAUSES
ACCOUNT FOR THE SHIFT

Now, for those who *disagree* with the shift, who think it is a terrible mistake, the most important thing, to begin with, is to understand how it came about. They need to understand that *it did not come about by discovery of how things actually are with morality and moral values.* Rather, that shift is the outcome of a long historical process that resulted in the disappearance of moral knowledge from Western societies. That is, it resulted in the *removal of the recognized values and principles of Christian/traditional moral understanding*—including its justifiable refinements and elaborations at the hands of great moral thinkers—*from the domain of the knowledge that must be taught by the knowledge institutions of Western society.* Instead, those values and principles were relocated, by subtle increments within a long drawn-out process, into the domain of *feelings* and *cultural traditions*, where they *could not* be taught by the acknowledged institutions of knowledge as a body of knowledge. This is what we mean when we speak here of the "disappearance of moral knowledge." It is this disappearance of moral knowledge that explains its unavailability as a resource for individual and group decision making in our time.

We must be clear that in speaking this way we do not mean to suggest that moral knowledge does not *exist.* Nor do we mean that no one has any moral knowledge. Claims to those effects are a part of the social process leading up to our present condition. But those claims were based upon a reinterpretation of knowledge itself that has by now proven to be neither plausible nor sustainable. Remember, from our previous discussions, that knowledge as it actually functions in real life (and it certainly does) is *the capacity to represent the relevant subject matter as it is on an appropriate basis of thought and experience.*

There indeed are many individuals and groups, past and present, who have or have had knowledge of the moral life, of good and evil, right and wrong, in this precise sense—not exhaustive knowledge, to be sure, but *extensive* and *substantial* knowledge nevertheless. Most of them have been quite unsophisticated people.[4] To say that moral knowledge has disappeared is just to say that what those people knew, and know now, is *no longer made available to the public as knowledge by the institutions of knowledge in our social and political system,* though it was so made available at times in the past.

But we must, further, be clear that this disappearance is *something that has actually happened.* If one does not understand this, much that now transpires in our public life and especially in our religious life will make no sense, because it will be approached upon the assumption that moral knowledge is still publicly available. The result will be confusion and paralysis. We are not dealing in this case with a conspiracy, but something much more powerful, a transformation so vast and pervasive that it is hard to bring it before the mind.

ELECTRICITY: A HELPFUL PARALLEL

To realize the significance of this change, one has to keep in mind the difference between whether knowledge of a particular subject is publicly available or not. As a simple but instructive illustration, consider the case of electricity and its production and application in homes and in industry. Although it remains true that no one really knows what electricity is in any *ultimate* sense, there is a vast body of knowledge about how it is produced and used. At one time that body of knowledge *did not exist,* and then, over a period of time, *it came into existence* and is still growing. That knowledge is now publicly available through recognized institutions of knowledge in our societies.

Because it is so available as a public resource, those who wish to acquire and use knowledge of electricity can do so. It can be taught, shared, tested for. On the basis of sharing it, people can work together in applying it, for example, to the wiring of a house, to an industrial operation, or in the invention of new technologies. Inspectors can check the applications to see if they are correctly and safely made. People can be qualified or disqualified for positions according to their knowledge of electricity. A social and economic order of vast proportions grows up around it. The outcome is a level of well-being, freedom, and comfort for individuals and society at large that is inconceivable apart from the shared, available knowledge—*not* just opinions, feelings, or traditions—about the production and use of electricity.

Now, one can easily draw up a scenario in which the knowledge of electricity "disappeared," that is, one where *the requisite knowledge institutions ceased to exist or function in making it publicly available to a wide range of people.* A fair-sized comet impacting the earth, a plague of some hitherto unknown type, or widespread use of "weapons of mass destruction" could have caused it. Or a superstitious and fanatical social movement or totalitarian government might have arisen that penalized the knowledge and use of electricity with death, severe injury, or deprivation. Electricity and those knowing how to set it up and use it would disappear from society.

Returning, now, to what we have labeled the "disappearance of moral knowledge," consider the original situation in which there was a—far from perfect, but still substantial—body of knowledge about moral good and evil, right and wrong. This knowledge was available to the public through the institutions of society recognized as sources of knowledge, primarily, of course, churches and schools (of all the various levels). Then, over a period of time, less than a century, the knowledge institutions of our society ceased, for various causes and reasons, to represent traditionally recognized moral values and principles as constituting a body of knowledge. They took it to be an area in which knowledge was not possible or not possible to the extent it could be taught as knowledge. This is the *disappearance of moral knowledge* that has actually occurred in our recent past.[5]

Now, the moral knowledge that disappeared was essentially Judeo-Christian or "biblical" in its origin and nature, though it involved contributions from classical (Greek and Roman) sources. Before the disappearance, Jesus Christ *was known* through his moral teachings, even by those who professed no special allegiance to him. It is safe to say that in Western circles he was recognized—the fulminations of a few aside—as the premier moral teacher of humanity.[6] It was basically moral principles stemming from him and his tradition that even *secular* thinkers of the 1800s and later attempted to reestablish on a nonreligious foundation. The failure of their project is one of the causes of the social relocation of morality outside of the domain of knowledge.

MULTIPLE CAUSES

But there is more to this causation than just the failure of that particular project—though *that* failure certainly proved to be very influential and continues to be so. Here we need to call attention to a number of other causal factors that led to the dismissal of the moral teachings of Jesus, in a refined form, from the domain of knowledge. Those concerned about knowledge of Christ in the modern world need to understand these factors.

First to be mentioned is the failure of the "visible" Christian church to apply the principles of Jesus to the appalling conditions of European humanity during the 1700s and 1800s. The church was the official, public custodian of morality during those centuries of great change in the conditions under which people were forced to live. If the church was the voice of Jesus to humankind, then he certainly appeared to have much to say that was terribly wrong and that sided with the ruling classes in horrible abuses of their power.

The discrediting of the church as a moral teacher and guide was accentuated by the advances of knowledge that came with the development of science and with the increased knowledge of the past and of other parts of the earth. These advances threatened the authority of the church at a more fundamental level. As widely interpreted, they called into question the basic documents—especially the Bible—and the founding events and personalities of Christian traditions and institutions. The initial result of all this was, as we have noted, not the rejection of Jesus Christ and of his core ethical teachings. Rather, it was an attempt to set those teachings on a secular, "scientific" basis and take them out of the hands of ecclesiastical authorities. That was the primary goal of most of the secular efforts just mentioned by well-known ethical thinkers of the 1700s and 1800s.

But their efforts in that direction simply were not found to be intellectually justifiable in the eyes of the learned world. That is the second major failure leading to our present situation with respect to the disappearance of moral knowledge. Like the first one, it is a matter of record, open to those willing to examine the facts of the case. Through much of this period, however, and well into the twentieth century, the "knowledge institutions" (churches and schools) of North America and Europe continued to present a "refined" Christian version of moral values and principles *as* knowledge of moral good and evil, right and wrong. You have only to look at the history of the academic world and the church and their institutions to see that this is so.[7] The failure at the intellectual level to find a secular, non-Christian basis in accepted knowledge for the values and principles of Christian morality—specifically, the central teachings of Jesus—took quite a long while to undermine the general confidence of the universities, and then of the churches, divinity schools, and seminaries, in the status of Christian ethics as knowledge of moral reality.

ANTHROPOLOGY AND PSYCHOLOGY

But eventually the lack of confidence in Christian morality as knowledge occurred, strongly taking hold of cultural institutions in the years immediately following World War II. However, a number of other factors contributed to that outcome. Most of these additional causal factors were side effects of the professionalization of higher education and of the elevation of its "research" as an independent source—perhaps the only socially recognized source—of knowledge. In particular, two powerful impulses against traditional moral knowledge originated from "research" in the developing fields of anthropology and psychology.

In anthropology the customs and practices of non-European peoples began, a century or so ago, to be studied for their own sakes—not just with a view to enlightening and correcting those peoples, much less of converting them. It had long been known that there were variations in moral practices from culture to culture across time and place. But the prevailing assumption was that non-European groups were grossly mistaken about moral matters. As those groups began to be taken seriously as subjects of research and academic studies, however, this assumption lost its grip. The reports coming back from research in "the field" seemed to indicate that the moralities of other cultures were *not* mistaken after all, but were just different. In some ways, the suggestion now was that they were even superior to European morality—with regard to general health and human flourishing, for example.

Moreover, seen from the viewpoint of these other cultures and the scholars studying them, the "European" and "Christian" morality was a product of just another culture with its own set of "folkways."[8] What had been taken by "us" to be moral knowledge was, then, just the product of one more historically conditioned culture with its own set of "folkways"—just one among many. And the various culturally specific "moralities," including "ours," obviously could not all be true, for they contradicted one another on many points. The conclusion drawn and made respectable by the academic world was that *none* were true and none constituted a body of moral knowledge.

The way of relieving the tension created by this (supposedly unbiased) examination of many cultures was to say that the question of knowledge (and truth) does not arise with reference to a "morality." This radically shifts the whole status of morality as such, as you can easily see. There are always moral *feelings* and moral *practices*, and these will never go away. They differ from culture to culture in virtue of varying conditions of living and the historical processes through which they arise. But there is no moral knowledge and no moral truth other than what is accepted as such by the particular group.[9] So it was thought.

This "solution" also could be extended, many advocated, to moral disagreements between individuals within a culture. Here too it could be said that different sentiments and practices do not imply that one *individual* has knowledge and truth while the other does not. Moral judgment, sentiment, and practice need not involve moral *knowledge* in any way. Moral divergences between cultures and moral disagreements between individuals, it came to be thought, are more easily dealt with and become less puzzling once knowledge and truth are simply taken off the table and out of play. They can be "explained" without reference to knowledge. The "disappearance of moral knowledge" seemed to resolve a range of thorny issues, and that marked it as a quite attractive and acceptable state of affairs.

THE DISAPPEARANCE OF THE HUMAN SELF OR SOUL

In roughly the same time period, developments in the emerging field of psychology came out at much the same place, though from a significantly different starting point. Efforts to turn psychology into a *science* that could be used as a basis for reliable prediction and control of human behavior took two main directions. One was in the development of "experimental" psychology. This kind of psychology attempted to study mental structures and processes—human consciousness and life, in part or in whole—solely in terms of the human body, often directly equating the mental with some aspects of the body. Today, following a tumultuous history, this approach to the human self lives on in the effort to treat all that is mental as processes in the brain.

The other main direction in psychology undertook to make it a science by way of the *unconscious*. Certainly that would be "science" of a very different sort, to say the least. Sigmund Freud was the most famous of those who sought to interpret human life and its moral dimensions in terms of the dynamics of psychological structures and processes that lie largely outside of the fields of conscious awareness, the most basic among which were what he called the id, the ego, and the superego (the primary locus of morality).

Now, from the origins of Western ethical thinking—in Socrates and Plato, shall we say, and in the Bible—it had been assumed that moral knowledge was knowledge of the human self or soul or of some of its most essential aspects. Whatever else may be said about these two powerful developments in psychology, they do not yield anything that could be subject to moral understanding, direction, and evaluation along traditional or commonsense lines of approach.

Yet under their influence, and that of a few less significant developments in psychology, the human being has been increasingly taken to be the kind of thing that could *not* be a subject of moral knowledge. That is because, in such views, the human self (if it even exists, which has been strongly denied) is governed by unconscious forces other than self-awareness and rational self-direction. The inner dynamics of a nonphysical "soul" or person responsibly weaving its own life together by choosing to follow rationally grounded moral insights or traditional teachings from the Bible disappeared from possible cognitive view—it was not thought to be "scientific"—and with it there disappeared the moral knowledge that had from the beginning taken such a *person* as its subject matter. Moral knowledge naturally disappears when its subject matter disappears.[10]

THREE LESS POWERFUL INFLUENCES

We have now located *four major causes of the elimination of moral knowledge from the knowledge institutions of our society.* These are: (1) the failure of the church to guide the development of modern societies into the ways of Jesus Christ; (2) the failure of modern thinkers and scholars to find a secular basis for Christian moral principles; (3) the emergence of many "moralities" at the hands of anthropological "research"; and (4) the disappearance of the human self at the hands of "advances" in psychology. In addition to these four powerful thrusts against the reality and availability of moral knowledge, however, there are several less profound, but still quite potent, forces that have arisen against it within the last century.

First, *moral standards have come to be regarded as mere displays of social and economic power, and those who employ them as blind or hypocritical.* There is no doubt, whatever you may make of them, that moral sentiments and moral appeals are very powerful, among the most powerful in human life. Because of this they can be, and often have been, used to manipulate people. A huge proportion of what goes into effective leadership depends upon moral appeals, and there is constant misuse of such appeals to gain conformity to the group and submission to leaders. Thus, from ancient times to the present, "conspiracy" theories of morality of one sort or another have been prominent. In such views there are no genuine moral values, and consequently there is no knowledge of them. Appeals to them are simply used to the advantage of those who would exercise power. Heady theories of how this works have long abounded within the academy. They are highly conjectural, to say the least, and almost totally without any basis in fact. But they are nevertheless highly influential.

Another contemporary impetus against moral knowledge is that *morality is actually harmful to any prospect of a full and free life.* This usually goes along with the idea that morality consists of a set of rules dealing with certain specific actions or situations, nonconformity to which justifies, in the eyes of society, the infliction of severe, irrational punishments. More popular than theoretical, this is the "just do it" approach to morality: just do it whether it makes any sense or not. History, art, and ordinary life are full of illustrations of abusive uses of such "morality"—more often than not a "morality" that has no real connection to what is truly good or evil, honorable or dishonorable. No doubt such uses need to be recognized as abusive and abolished. Indeed, that is a clearly moral imperative.

On the other hand, there are theoretical views that say suppression of desire is bad for your mental and physical health. Strongly associated with Freudianism in the twentieth century, this outlook is a part of the relentless modern drive toward hedonism and against the good. And it is true that an essential role of morality in human life is to give us a place to stand *against* desires and pleasures. Hence it must be able to suppress or redirect desire. It must enable us to do what we do not (for the moment at least) want to do, and to not do what we at the moment want to do. Apart from this, morality is largely pointless. Morality is a good and necessary thing, and it must be based upon genuine knowledge of what is good.

However, we must grant that more specific *rules* of what is contextually accepted as morality are often turned *against* what is truly good, not just against what is only desired. Usually it is at the hands of people with some degree of power. This misuse succeeds precisely because moral sentiments and appeals are so powerful. Constant vigilance based upon good understanding—indeed, upon knowledge—of moral values and the moral life is required to prevent this from happening. *Jesus himself is the master*

of critiquing the misguided use of "moral" rules against what is good.
Thus his frequent emphasis upon the harm and futility arising
from "the 'righteousness' of the scribes and Pharisees." But criticisms made of the abuse of morality, far from ruling out moral
knowledge, are usually made upon the basis of genuine moral
insight. So those criticisms cannot be an argument *against* the
reality and use of moral knowledge.

A third element in the rejection of moral knowledge is really
directed against the nature and function of knowledge itself.
Knowledge itself is said by many today to be oppressive. Anything that
is allowed to stand as knowledge is something you *must* come to
terms with—if not because you respect it as such in the guidance
of your life, then at least because others do and will not leave you
alone to disregard it. Knowledge, as we have noted, confers rights
to act and to direct action, to set policy and direct its implementa-
tion, and to teach. It does this in a way that neither feeling, opinion, tradition, nor mere power ever do. That proves to be highly
threatening to some primary values of contemporary Western life,
especially to self-determination and freedom from social domina-
tion, for example—the "freedom" to do "what I want to do."

But in fact others can, on the basis of knowledge, tell you what
to do. (Sounds ominous, doesn't it!) That is the nature of knowledge, and it is all the more "threatening" in the moral realm. It
would mean you or I could—selectively at least—be *imposed upon.*
We say, "Don't impose your opinions on me," but not "Don't
impose your knowledge on me," though of course the imposition
of knowledge can be done in a wrong way. People ("experts") can
even have a moral obligation to "impose" knowledge in certain
cases. Contemporary individuals like to say that no one has a *right*
to tell them what to do or think. But the possession of knowledge
does confer precisely that right in suitable circumstances. That
is one reason why "enlightened" people today are very guarded
against knowledge and against truth generally.

FREEDOM AND "FEELING GOOD"

It has become an unquestioned moral assumption of most Western cultures, and certainly of North American ones, that people should be *free*. What that means in the popular mind and popular culture is that people should be permitted, if not actually enabled, to do what they want. This is almost always joined with the assumption that what people do want is to enjoy *pleasure*. Sometimes they speak of "happiness," but that term has little meaning to most folks other than *feeling good*.[11]

So it is now generally thought that desiring to do something is a sufficient or at least a weighty reason for doing it. From this we get our overall culture of *sensuality*, in which people are almost totally governed by their feelings. Within that context the major ills of contemporary life fall readily into place: everything from obesity to elder abuse, from broken families with broken lives to drug dependency and addiction, from misuse of credit to contempt and animosities between racial and other groups. Over these we helplessly chant our slogans such as "choice," "diversity" and "tolerance," hoping the grim and grinding realities will go away.[12] These ills are natural outcomes of a culture that finds the saying "If it feels good, do it" humorous instead of morally ridiculous or shameful.

So there is a constellation of causal factors that explains why moral knowledge has disappeared as a resource for living and is not made publicly available from our institutions of knowledge. It is easy to understand how the knowledge institutions (churches and schools) would give in to the tremendous pressure of these factors. But we still must keep it clear that these *causes*, individually or all together, do *not* provide a *good reason* for rejecting moral knowledge or for not making it available through relevant social institutions. No one has demonstrated or proved that there is no moral reality[13] or no teachable knowledge of it, or that it *should not* be taught as such by our institutions. The disappearance of moral knowledge is simply a social condition into which the United States and most of the West has drifted. The "secular" university, as it arose, fell heir to the task of moral education and simply could not handle it. It had no resources for it and has now haughtily disowned the task—while surreptitiously continuing to *practice* a mercilessly rigorous moral system free from rational scrutiny in the public forum of ideas.

CONTINUING RECOGNITION THAT LOVE, CARE FOR HUMAN GOOD, IS THE CENTER OF ETHICAL LIVING

So let us now think a little more deeply concerning *what moral knowledge is knowledge of* in the tradition of Jesus. To this end we go back to Habermas's statement that the major points of modern moral understanding are the direct descendants or "heirs" of "the Judaic ethic of justice and the Christian ethic of love." Surely he is right, but what does it mean?

We might begin by pointing out that there is a natural connection and a certain priority to be observed between justice and love. Justice without love will *always* fall short of what needs to be done. It will never be as good as it should be. Justice without love will never do justice to justice, nor will "love" without justice ever do justice to love. Indeed, it will not be love at all; for *love wills the good of what is loved,* and that must include justice where justice is lacking. Justice is a fundamental human good and a prerequisite of many others. The correct understanding of love, and the intelligent overall orientation of our lives in terms of it, is the source from which all standards of virtue and right behavior and all the aspects of goodness of character coherently flow. That is certainly the view of Jesus and the New Testament, and in that view love is *everything.*[14]

SOME CONTEMPORARY STATEMENTS

Let us see how that view of love looks in the thin atmosphere of contemporary philosophy. A well-known contemporary writer on ethics, Simon Blackburn, has written a book called *Being Good*. In it he says shared feelings or "passions" provide the common point of view that enables us to give and receive reasons that morally justify or condemn actions and characters. The common passions are what "enable common humanity to go forward." But which passions? "The foundations of moral motivation are not the procedural rules on a kind of discourse," he says, "but the feelings to which we can rise. As Confucius saw long ago, benevolence or concern for humanity is the indispensable root of it all."[15]

There is something a little odd about this statement. Why not Jesus instead of Confucius? Confucius certainly was a great man and should be honored as such. But he is not exactly a fountainhead of civilizations based upon benevolence. This author, like most sophisticates of today, cannot say "love" and he cannot say "Jesus." Odd, but revealing of where we now stand. Love, of course, goes *far* beyond benevolence (as in the phrase "a benevolent society"). And Jesus is the man whom love put on the cross, establishing a meaning for love that benevolence and charity do not come close to. Still, if informed people were asked to name a famous and influential advocate of benevolence, "Confucius" would not be the first name on their lips.

With the fundamental insight into the primacy of benevolence under his belt, this author proceeds to ask the question: "So is there such a thing as moral knowledge?" And he replies: "Fortunately, there are countless small, unpretentious things that we know with perfect certainty. Happiness is preferable to misery, and dignity is better than humiliation. It is bad that people suffer, and worse if a culture turns a blind eye to their suffering. Death is worse than life; the attempt to find a common point of view is better than manipulative contempt for it."[16] Though this author does not say as much, these "things that we know with perfect certainty" are surely to be seen as more specific cases for the application of "benevolence or concern for humanity . . . the indispensable root of it all." Acting to promote happiness and eliminate misery or to protect dignity is morally good, dutiful, and right, because they are cases of benevolence or, better, of love. And no doubt we know that. No doubt that knowledge is exactly what Jesus affirms, and affirms with a clarity and an effect of no other in human history.

Another highly regarded contemporary writer, Hilary Putnam, states: "'Ethics' is present in all human cultures because in all cultures there are individuals prepared to sacrifice for the survival of the community. The human capacity for loyalty to something larger than the individual, something at least as large as the community, is indeed a *presupposition* of ethics."[17] He continues: "The emphasis on alleviating suffering regardless of the class or gender of the sufferer . . . has deep roots in the great religious traditions of the world," and that emphasis is what he chooses to "refer to by the name of ethics." He a little later refers with agreement to the view of Emmanuel Levinas that "the irreducible foundation of ethics is *my* immediate recognition, when confronted with a suffering fellow human being, that *I* have an obligation to do something. . . . Not to feel the obligation to help the sufferer at all, not to recognize that if I can, I *must* help, or to feel that obligation only when the suffering person I am confronted with is *nice,* or *sympathetic,* or *someone I can identify with,* is not to be ethical at all, no matter how many principles one may be guided by or willing to give one's life for."[18]

In fact, this author says, "What I shall call 'ethics' is precisely the morality that Nietzsche deplored and regarded as a weakness or even a sickness." As Nietzsche ceaselessly emphasized, that is the fundamentally *Christian* ethic, and it has, as we have seen above, been pushed out of the category of teachable knowledge—no longer to be conveyed as knowledge by the "knowledge institutions" of North America and Europe. It is precisely *that* moral knowledge that has now "disappeared." But does Christ still make himself present at the most elevated levels of modern thought? Yes, and intellectually careful people know that it is so, even if they will not or cannot speak his name or use his word, "love."

It is not as if Christ alone knew or taught that love ("benevolence," "compassion") is the center of what is right, obligatory, and good among human beings. It is indeed an "open secret"—something that everyone deep down knows, if they will but carefully consider it. But they are wary of him and of love, perhaps because they do not know how to meet his demands or the demands of love in real life. Everyone knows the evil of intent to harm and the goodness of intent to help, to benefit. Good and evil are by and large immediately sensed, and they further reveal themselves to reflection and theoretical elaboration. This perception of good and evil is the fundamental intuition of the moral life, and it is given even to small children and unsophisticates of all levels, though they may be unable to articulate or defend it.

JESUS AND THE NATURE OF *AGAPE* LOVE

Though the centrality of love to duty and virtue is not unique to Jesus and his people, exactly what it means—how it is to be elaborated in thought and institution, and how it is to be put into individual practice—is another matter altogether, and the love of which Jesus speaks contains many unique elements. They are developed and exemplified in the history of his people.

For one thing, there is a distinctive emphasis by Jesus on loving your *neighbor*, your "near dweller," not upon loving "humanity" or "everyone."[19] What this means is that our duty and our virtue is *to love those with whom we are in effectual contact*—those we can really do something about. Usually, though not always, they will be people near to us, *nigh* to us, in physical proximity to us. Now, this was not a completely new teaching, though its profound meaning was usually missed—a point of which Jesus made much in numerous ways. The teachers of his day knew of it and taught it, of course, in conjunction with the "Hear, O Israel" of Deuteronomy 6:4–5. When Jesus on one occasion responds to a scholar's question about the foremost commandment, he replies with two commandments, joining love of neighbor to love of God. The scholar agrees and repeats both, calling them "more important than all whole burnt offerings and sacrifices" (Mark 12:28–33).

The command of neighbor love is explicitly stated in an unobtrusive passage of the Old Testament. Leviticus 19:18 directs God's people not to take revenge or to hold a grudge—not carry an evil intent—against their fellow Jews, "their people": "but you shall love your neighbor as yourself." This is the exact language Jesus uses in Mark 12:31 to reply to the scholar testing him. But then the same chapter in Leviticus proceeds to recognize a problem. The people addressed would have "neighbors" other than their fellow Jews. In one of the most profound and startling statements in all of the Bible, God's chosen people are told: "The alien who resides with you shall be to you as the citizen among you, and you shall love the alien as yourself, for you were aliens in the land of Egypt" (19:34). That is, they knew the painful existence of those who are excluded from the "power people," and love toward others who were excluded in the same situation was the reasonable moral response—no doubt a love intended to bring justice with it. The fact that aliens were "other" did not change the moral obligation.

And Jesus himself was always reaching out in love to the "outsiders" who were "nigh" to him. It made no difference to him if they were marked as "unclean" in one or more of the several senses of "unclean" defined and enforced by the "proper people" of his day. Gentiles, Samaritans, people with nasty diseases, prostitutes, and the demon-possessed came "nigh" to him and he to them, and he accepted them and loved them, helping them in ways he could.

THE "ORDINARINESS" OF JESUS'S KIND OF LOVE

The "love" Jesus lived and taught, however, is not limited to compassion for the suffering and the downtrodden. Those were simple and obvious cases of love, to be sure: obvious because the needs of such people were so glaring, and because they were not the usual objects of love for ordinary people in ordinary life. They tended to be passed by. Helping people in dire need was recognized as a "big deal," something to make a show of, and as a praiseworthy thing for *extraordinary* people to do—rather as we today would describe someone as a "philanthropist." Unfortunately, people are not thought to be philanthropists because they are kind and thoughtful and look out for the good of those around them and serve them. But when Jesus speaks of love as the principle of life as it ought to be, he is referring mainly to the posture of *benefiting others in the ordinary relations of ordinary life*. The heroic occasions will then fit in as they come along, but the reverse is not true.

Thus, for example, his washing of the feet of the apostles at the Last Supper (John 13:3–15) was a simple act of loving them. The feet needed to be washed, but none of the apostles were going to do it, though they were well aware of the need and the custom. He then told them to follow his example and wash one another's feet (v. 14).[20] The reality of his new community of love was that "the greatest among you will be your servant" (Matt. 23:11), and he set the pattern, saying, "I am among you as one who serves" (Luke 22:27).

The love of which Jesus speaks addresses the provision of *positive* goods, not just alleviation of painful conditions. This and the difference it makes are often missed by those who like to compare the teachings of Jesus to those of other religions. Our aim here is not to prove that Jesus is superior to other spiritual masters and traditions. But he really *is* different, and we should acknowledge it. Commonly, "Do not do to others what you would not have them do to you," the Silver Rule, is equated with, "Do to others as you would have them do to you," the Golden Rule, but they are vastly different in application.

The positive formulation is directed toward helping others by doing what is good for them. The negative formulation is directed toward avoiding harm. It might be that some, in practice, would do the same things under either formulation, but many would not. The Silver Rule is not directed toward the good of the other the way the Golden Rule is. The mind and heart are in a different place for those who would follow one or the other. The Golden Rule is devoted to the good in the lives of those around us, and this reaches far beyond the mere absence of harm. The "love" of Jesus not only reaches indiscriminately toward those with whom we are actually in contact, but it aspires toward a remarkable richness in their lives, not simply the alleviation of their suffering. Thus it is much more than compassion.

LOVE AND THE "LAW"

Now, once we begin to understand the "love" coming from Jesus, we can see where neighbor love was in fact present in the "law" of the tradition into which he was born. (Psalm 119 tries to do justice to the majesty, beauty and goodness of the law of the Lord.) Jesus himself said that if you treat people around you as you want them to treat you, "this is the law and the prophets" (Matt. 7:12). That means that if you do the good for others that you want them to do for you, then doing what was taught as good and right by the moral dimension of the Mosaic law (the Ten Commandments, etc.) and by the Old Testament prophets will be a natural side effect, an automatic outcome.

This teaching continued to develop in the early Christian church. Paul says bluntly: "The one who loves another has fulfilled the law. The commandments, 'You shall not commit adultery; You shall not murder; You shall not steal; You shall not covet'; and any other commandment, are summed up in this word, 'Love your neighbor as yourself.' Love does no wrong to a neighbor; therefore, love is the fulfilling of the law" (Rom. 13:8–10). Moral rules are subordinate to the moral attitude or disposition of love. Of course, love is also much more than the fulfillment of the law. Peter, James, and John all echo this thought of the centrality and sufficiency of love.

The sad truth is, on the other hand, that law is not sufficient for love. Taken alone, it has a built-in deficiency. Love is open-ended toward human good in a way law is not. Love is *covenantal*, while law is *contractual*, defining limitations of obligation. You can keep the law as divinely formulated *without* loving your neighbor or even yourself. Religion and culture as well as individuals are constantly busy finding ways to do that. Our current "Christian" cultures, often along "denominational" lines, are deeply involved in such a project. It is one of the things that defeats the purposes of Christ in them, generation after generation. They are cursed with a loveless, heartless "righteousness," always taking a specific cultural form that defines an "us" and a "them" who can be treated with something less than love, even with contemptuous violence. Jesus's Sermon on the Mount, especially from Matthew 5:20 onward, is chiefly directed against this deadly tendency toward outward observance in the religious and cultural life.

LOVE AND VIRTUES

The practice and understanding of love that emerges in Jesus and develops in his people over centuries essentially involves a cloud of other human traits or conditions without which it cannot be love fully formed. We see this in lists that show up here and there in the New Testament and in the spiritual literature that develops in the church through the ages. For example, in Colossians 3 we find listed: constant focus upon Christ and God (vv. 1–4); truthfulness (v. 9); viewing all kinds of people as God sees them ("inclusively," vv. 10–11); compassion, kindness, humility, gentleness, patience (v. 12); and forbearance and forgiveness (v. 13). And capping off this list, as in other passages, is *agape* love (v. 14; see also Rom. 5:5; 2 Pet. 1:7).

In Galatians 5 the list given is of components in the fruit (one fruit) of the Spirit: "love, joy, peace, patience, kindness, generosity, faithfulness, gentleness, and self-control" (vv. 22–23). In 1 Corinthians 13, most famously perhaps, we get a list of things that you can have without love—humanly admirable things, no doubt, but of no moral value when unaccompanied by love (vv. 1–3)—and then a list of acts and character traits that genuine love brings with it into our life: "Love is patient; love is kind; love is not envious or boastful or arrogant or rude. It does not insist on its own way; it is not irritable or resentful; it does not rejoice in wrongdoing, but rejoices in the truth. It bears all things, believes all things, hopes all things, endures all things. Love never ends" (vv. 4–8).

With that we can see that the love of which Jesus speaks as the teacher of nations is no small thing. It cannot be an occasional distinct act of will that we "add on" to a life unformed by it. We can also see why, returning to some previous comments, "Christian civilization"—a phrase that can be used only with certain misgivings—failed so miserably by its own standards during the great periods of colonization, industrialization, and technological development out of which the world of the twentieth and twenty-first centuries arose.

CAN LOVE BE TRUSTED?

The root of the failure, then as now, is unwillingness to submit human desire, especially as it masters groups of people,[21] to what is good as indicated by love. Jesus addresses this fundamental problem in his saying: "Those who want to save their life will lose it" (Mark 8:35). One of our contemporary thinkers quoted above says, "In all human cultures there are individuals prepared to sacrifice for the survival of the community. The human capacity for loyalty to something larger than the individual, something at least as large as the community, is indeed a *presupposition* of ethics." He means that the readiness to sacrifice is a presupposition of *ethical living*, of being a good person, not of ethics as an academic or intellectual project. You can't succeed in being ethical in act or character *unless you have abandoned having your way, fulfilling your own desires, as the rule of your life.* That is the ethical meaning of love in real life as taught and practiced by Jesus. It leaves us with the question: Who will take care of us?

The dark truth is that we may praise love (or, more weakly, "benevolence" or "compassion"), and few people would refuse to do so when love is rightly understood. We may wish to be loving—to be kind and helpful in our relations to those near us. But we do not trust love, and we think it could easily ruin our carefully guarded hold on life. We are frightened of the world we are in, and that makes us angry and hostile, and contempt makes it easier to harm or disregard the good of others. So the world boils with contempt. The more refined the human setting, the more fine-tuned the contempt.

You don't have to know that God exists and that Jesus is for real to know that love is the good and the right for human beings. It is laughably false to say that if there is no God, everything is permitted, provided everything else remains as we now know it to be. It takes little intelligence to know that to live in love is the morally good and right way to live. But entering into and growing in love—actually being it and doing it in the context of real life—is quite another matter. Many misunderstandings of what love is have to be worked through before one can come to peace in it. Evil has a vested interest in confusing and distorting love.

Above all, one has to find by thought and experience that love can be trusted as a way of life. This can be learned by interaction with Jesus in all ordinary and extraordinary circumstances. (More about this later.) He can bring it to pass that we rely on love; and that is why he boldly asserted that the *only* mark of being his student or apprentice in life was how his students love one another (John 13:35). And it is, again, why one of his best students could say, on the basis of a lifetime of experience: "Everyone who loves is born of God and knows God" (1 John 4:7). Love is not God, but God is love. It is who he is, his very identity. And our world under a God like that is a place where it is safe to do and be what is good and what is right. Living in love as Jesus defines it by his words and deeds is the sure way to know Christ in the modern world.[22] On the other hand, if you are not reconciled to living in love as the center of your life, and *actually* living that way, any knowledge you may have of Christ will be shallow and shaky at best.

FOR DISCUSSION

1. What is the reality of Christ's influence on the understanding of the moral life, the understanding of moral good and evil, right and wrong? In North America?

2. What has changed during the recent past in the popular understanding of good and evil, right and wrong?

3. "The triumph of desire over good at the public level." Does this accurately describe life in Western societies today?

4. Can you make sense of the distinction between *reasons* for a change in attitude toward good and evil and *causes* of that change?

5. What is the "disappearance of moral knowledge"? Has it actually happened?

6. Is the parallel with the possible disappearance of knowledge of *electricity* accurate? Is it helpful in understanding the disappearance of moral knowledge?

7. Of the listed *causes* of the disappearance of accepted knowledge of good and evil, right and wrong, which do you think has been the most influential?

8. Is love still implicitly recognized as the center of moral goodness and ethical living? That is, is it the center of what marks someone as a "really good person"? What might be some alternatives offered today? Keeping the rules?

9. Consider: "Justice without love will never do justice to justice."

10. In what ways do the teachings of Jesus carry us far beyond contemporary understandings of love? Beyond compassion?

11. Why is law not enough to constitute love? How does virtue go beyond law?

12. Why do you think Jesus chose "love of one another" as the mark of his disciples or students (John 13:35)?

FOUR

Can We Know That God Exists?

On the Way Back to Christ

May grace and peace be yours in abundance in the
knowledge of God and of Jesus our Lord.

PETER, 2 PETER 1:2

I S IT POSSIBLE to *know* that God exists? This question is
central to our work here, for knowledge of God is what Christ
is primarily about. "He is the image of the invisible God," was
the language of the apostle Paul (Col. 1:15), and he himself is
recorded as saying, "Whoever has seen me has seen the Father"
(John 14:9). It was his scandalous claim that "no one knows . . .
who the Father is except the Son and anyone to whom the Son
chooses to reveal him" (Luke 10:22; Matt. 11:27). His early followers were described as those who "through him . . . have come
to trust in God, who raised him from the dead and gave him
glory, so that . . . faith and hope are set on God" (1 Pet. 1:21).

If there is no God, or if knowledge of God is impossible (as
it certainly would be if there is no God), what is left of "Christ"
is really nothing at all—or worse still, it is a huge deception. It
might still be something impressive or inspiring on a human
scale, for on that scale who really stands higher than Christ? But
it could not then be redemptive of the torn and hapless human

condition. He would be just another "gentle cynic" as some of our "Jesus scholars" now say. So our first order of business now is to deal with the challenging and timeworn issue of the existence of God.

First of all, who is the God we are talking about? In thinking of God today we do not start from zero, but from within rich conceptions that have come down to us from the past. In this world there are, no doubt, many ways of thinking about God, but the "God" of which we here speak is the God of traditional Western theology. He is defined by the *biblical* traditions of Judaism and Christianity and the understanding of his nature has been elaborated by many thoughtful people in those traditions up to the present. *That* God, as is well known, is a spiritual or nonphysical being with the attributes of personality: consciousness, knowledge, emotion, and will. He is a *person* of immense proportions in substance, power, and goodness of character, who, because of his basic nature as love, creates and involves himself in human affairs. His own existence and activities depend upon nothing other than himself, unless he so chooses. In this sense he is an ultimate and absolute personal being.[1]

God thus understood communicates and makes covenant with human beings in ways most suitable to his purposes for them in creation. Such is the God of the biblical tradition and the God whom Jesus taught us to call "Father." In a manner unique to Jesus among all teachers of the earth, he tells us that we can, right now, right where we are, rely upon the "kingdom" of this God—upon his rule, reign, or governance—and that we will then, by experience, find that "kingdom" to have the character of a loving *family* in its most ideal form.

THE BIBLICAL VISION OF GOD

The above picture of God stands out strongly and clearly in how he acts in the biblical stories and how he is addressed in biblical prayers. It pulsates in the biblical "hymnbook" we call Psalms and is exemplified in the great corporate prayer of the Israelites in Nehemiah 9:6–37. There, who God-Jehovah is and what he is like are described in terms of what he has done: "You are the Lord, you alone; you have made the heavens, the heaven of the heavens, with all their host, the earth and all that is on it, the seas and all that is in them. To all of them you give life, and the host of heaven worships you" (v. 6). Then there is an almost seamless shift of focus in the prayer to God's particular communications, his covenant making, and his special provisions for the Jewish people: "You are the Lord, the God who chose Abram and brought him out of Ur of the Chaldeans and gave him the name Abraham; and you found his heart faithful before you, and made with him a covenant to give to his descendants the land of the Canaanite. . . . And you have fulfilled your promise, for you are righteous" (vv. 7–8). The prayer goes on to recite outstanding details in the history of the Israelites and in God's interventions to sustain them, chastise them, and draw them forward in his purposes in human history.

This quite "standard" approach to God in biblical praying is largely repeated and updated to include Jesus and his followers in Acts 4:24–31. Here the Lord as creator again forms the background of the prayer, and his interventions into the affairs of his chosen people are cited and further sought in the circumstances of persecution of the earliest followers of Christ. The context of this passage is one in which there are ongoing divine interventions in and on behalf of the group of disciples of Jesus.[2]

If there is such a God as this, it obviously has tremendous implications for "worldview" issues and for individual lives—that is, it makes a huge difference in how we can and should live. A God who is responsible for our existence and intervenes in our lives certainly has some purpose for us to serve and has significant claims upon us and our behavior. That will mean that humanity is not, ultimately, in charge and not free simply to do as it wishes and as it can. Some people will find this to be a good thing, while others will bitterly resent it. Similarly, some will find great peace and joy in the idea that such a God cares for them and for his creation and that he will see to it that they are safe in his hands. Others will find ceaseless fault with how he is doing his "job" and will rebel against the very idea of such a God. Those are the human reactions.

The existence and nature of God, however, are entirely indifferent to what we may or may not think or wish. They have that in common with all but, possibly, a very few matters of fact. The facts and laws of physics or history, for example, are totally indifferent to what we may think or feel about them. It is the same with whatever facts and laws there may be beyond the physical, in the spiritual or other worlds. So we turn now to the question of whether such a God as we here have in mind can be known to exist. If he can be known to exist, he of course exists, and it would then seem highly likely that such a God would intervene in human affairs. In the remainder of this chapter we will deal with the "existence" side of the question, reserving the "intervention" side for later chapters.

IMPRESSIONS OF GOD'S EXISTENCE

There is no reason in the nature of things why such a God could not exist or should not exist. There is nothing about the "realm of nature" that renders this God impossible, improbable, or implausible. More generally still, if we start from nothing in our thinking, there is no reason why any one type of thing rather than another should or should not exist. This is what earlier writers used to call the "antecedent credibility" of theism or of God. Certainly the existence of the God we are talking about here is *no more* inherently incredible than would be the existence of the physical universe on its own.

Indications that there is a God come from two main sources: (1) the natural world around us—the physical universe we will call it—and (2) peculiar types of experiences that individuals have within certain forms of life. The biblical and the classical sources out of which our contemporary ways of thinking about God arise *take the physical universe to be conclusive evidence for the existence of God.* Familiar words from the Bible show this: "In the beginning God created the heavens and the earth" (Gen. 1:1). "O Lord, our Sovereign, how majestic is your name in all the earth! You have set your glory above the heavens. . . . I look at your heavens, the work of your fingers, the moon and the stars that you have established" (Ps. 8:1–3). "The heavens are telling of the glory of God; and the firmament proclaims his handiwork. Day to day pours forth speech, and night to night declares knowledge" (Ps. 19:1–2).

No doubt the strongest biblical statement on the point here at issue comes from Paul. He states: "What can be known about God is plain to them, because God has shown it to them. Ever since the creation of the world *his eternal power and divine nature, invisible though they are, have been understood and seen through the things he has made.* So they are without excuse" (Rom. 1:19–20).

On the classical side, in Greek texts, the earliest thorough expression of this same line of thought comes from the fourth century BCE in Plato's *Laws.*[3] There, as elsewhere in Plato, a nonphysical reality called "soul" is treated as the divine source of "motion" (meaning *change*) in the physical universe. A little later in this same century, Plato's most famous student, Aristotle, developed a refined version of this view. In Book 12 of his *Metaphysics* he explains that the ultimate or "prime" mover of the universe is a personal being—pure thought—that does not itself change ("move"), but directly or indirectly "moves" everything else through the attraction of its own radiant magnificence. According to him, the changing universe depends for its nature upon "One who changeth not."

Epictetus, a famous Stoic philosopher contemporary to Paul, assigned the pervasive order in physical reality to the goodwill of God or "Providence": "From the very construction of a complete work, we are used to declare positively that it must be the operation of some artificer, and not the effect of mere chance. Does every such work then demonstrate an artificer, and visible objects not do so?" Is not the order in things, an order obvious to thought, "sufficient to prevail on men and make them ashamed of leaving an artificer out of their scheme? . . . Let them explain to us . . . how it is possible that things so wonderful, and which carry such marks of contrivance, should come to pass spontaneously and without design."[4]

The almost irresistible impression of a "maker" of the physical universe is no doubt what Paul was referring to when he claimed that the existence and nature of God was "plain" or "shown" to humans. This impression remains very strong up to today. David Hume, often thought to be the prince of modern skeptics, conceded: "The whole frame of nature bespeaks an intelligent author; and no rational enquirer can, after serious reflection, suspend his belief a moment with regard to the primary principles of genuine Theism and Religion."[5] This same outlook survives in the later, carefully guarded concession of Hume's "Philo," in the posthumously published *Dialogues Concerning Natural Religion*, "That the cause or causes of order in the universe probably bear some remote analogy to human intelligence."[6]

Misunderstandings of Darwin's theory of "natural selection" have in more recent times blunted the impact of the reasoning behind this conclusion in the minds of people generally. But in recent years an increased understanding of the astonishing complexity of life has led some who were longtime atheists to reconsider their position.[7] In any case, the complexity and order of the physical universe reaches far beyond, and is prior to, the complexity of *living* beings, to which Darwin's theory applies; and that prior order would have been there even if life and evolution had never occurred. (Of course, *we*, then, would know nothing about it or about anything else!)

A CLOSER LOOK AT THE REASONING

This much, then, indicates the power of awareness of the physical universe to generate belief in God. But the mere power of impressions can generate beliefs that are false. Beliefs that the earth is flat and that the sun travels around it are cases in point. So we need to see whether and to what extent the existence and nature of the physical universe actually provide us with *knowledge* that there is some such God as is here in question. We want to say immediately that it at least carries us a long way in that direction. How so?

First, there was a *beginning* of the physical universe. That now seems to be an established fact, though it was long denied. It is now a part of accepted physical theory that the physical universe *was not* and then it *was*. It *originated* with what is widely known as the "big bang." (Of course, in no ordinary sense was it big or a bang. Rather, bigness and bangness can come only later, according to the accepted scientific theory.) From what we now understand of the physical order there must have been such an event, and a certain type of "background radiation" now detectable is thought to be a result of it.[8]

If this is so, we are faced with a stark alternative. *Either* the physical universe was not produced by anything *or* it was produced by something that is not physical—something spiritual in that minimal sense. The former cannot be, so the latter is the case.

The former cannot be because every physical thing or process, from galaxies to molecules, certainly arises out of something else. At the very minimum, every constituent of the physical world about us comes into existence in a *context* of other physical things, not in a context of nothing. Is the physical world as a whole an exception to this general rule? Consider the physical contents of any area in space—your house or apartment, for example. They all will have come to be from events and things other than themselves. Now enlarge the area to any extent you please—your street or town, for example—and that will still be true. The solar system containing our planet earth arose out of a prior condition in and around it several billion years after the "big bang." Similarly for our galaxy, the Milky Way, and for clusters of galaxies.

Although it is difficult to imagine or conceptualize the whole of the physical universe, there is at the very least no reason to think that this requirement of a prior causal condition or "source" does not apply to it as well. And there is good reason to think it does apply, for it too is a *physical* reality. Since we are speaking, at this point, of the origination of the physical universe as a whole, its causal source obviously will not be physical. Accordingly it was brought into existence by something that is *not* physical, by something "spiritual" at least in that negative sense.

NO "CAUSAL CLOSURE" OF THE PHYSICAL

Physical realities are of an essentially dependent nature. That is obvious from any careful consideration of them. This is what eliminates the alternative that the physical universe had no cause at all. There is a principle that many investigators accept as a truth guiding the investigation of nature. It holds that *every* physical event has a *physical* cause. This is called the "causal closure" of the physical domain. It is a sensible, practical rule that, when involved in investigations of physical phenomena, we should look for physical causes. (In "research" it could still be a good rule to look only for physical or at least "nonsupernatural" causes of physical things and events, but without any dogmatic assumptions about reality as a whole, or about what *must* be the case in the physical universe.) But to take this rule as a *practical* guide for individual investigations is not the same as asserting the "causal closure" of the whole physical domain; namely, that *every* physical event or thing has a *physical cause*.

To accept the view that there was nothing and then there was the physical universe in the incipient stage of its development is certainly to *reject* the causal closure of the physical universe. Then we do have something physical with no physical cause—the physical universe itself. *No* cause is certainly, whatever else, no *physical* cause. And it follows that the physical universe as a whole is not totally subject to physical causation. This well may leave one wondering why all physical events *in* the physical universe would have to have only physical causes. If you allow that the entire physical universe originated "from nothing," then there is no reason why physical things and events would not continue to arise "from nothing." If the entire universe could originate from nothing, then surely a cup of tea could originate from nothing.

ATTEMPTED EVASIONS

One way you might hope to evade the conclusion that the physical universe is brought into existence by something that is not physical is to say that the physical universe itself is not actually physical, but is in some sense "spiritual." Now this attempt has been made in various ways, by thinkers Eastern and Western.[9] Following it, the essentially dependent nature of the physical universe might seem to be avoided. It would then not itself be physical as a whole, and it might be treated as sufficient unto itself—a traditional mark of divinity—and as not requiring a cause.

But there are a number of difficulties with this approach. First, contrary to what is now taken to be a fact, according to it the physical universe does not have a beginning and is not the kind of thing that requires one. That seems now refuted. Second, to take this position amounts to assigning some traditional attributes of deity to the physical universe itself. Third, that being true, to take this path is to "give up the game," to admit defeat so far as most current opponents of "God" and the knowledge of God are concerned. It does have one advantage, so far as those opponents are concerned—the divinization of physical nature avoids the burdens of living in a world presided over by a *personal* God to whom they are responsible. This is something greatly desired by many people today who still want to be "spiritual" and gain some benefits thereof. They are often very sophisticated and intelligent people who do not wish to answer to anyone for their life or be accountable to God. Evading this is also a benefit of much "New Age" spirituality, earlier called the "Nirvana story."

But the lines of reasoning that support this view of a self-sufficient physical universe, though very ancient, are extremely hard to sustain logically. They usually wind up not explaining the physical universe at all, but explaining it away in one sense or another as not being "real." And for most of those who engage in such theories they are purely ad hoc attempts to avoid "traditional" religion while remaining "spiritual." That is to say, their only motivation for accepting those lines of reasoning, which conclude the physical universe itself to be "spiritual," is that they allow them (to their own minds, at least) to remain "spiritual" without any need of a "god." There is no separate line of reasoning that leads to a self-sufficing physical world.

Another way of trying to avoid the conclusion that there is a nonphysical being ("God") who created the physical universe is to point out that the scientific theory that the physical universe has a beginning is, after all, *only* a scientific theory. Scientific theories change, we know. Perhaps at some point the physical theories that give us the "big bang" will be abandoned. Rather than argue this point, which is basically solid, we now point out that there are other long-standing reasons for thinking that the physical world has a beginning, however remote in time it may be.[10]

THE CAUSAL SERIES OF THE PHYSICAL
UNIVERSE MUST HAVE A FIRST MEMBER

Any event or condition in the physical world, from the falling of that leaf from this tree to a time slice of the entire physical universe—its total condition at a given point in time—comes about as the result of a *series of causes* leading up to it. That series must be *completed* at the point where the condition or event in question is present. If any of its causal conditions (its necessary conditions) had *not* transpired by that point, then that event would not occur. Since it occurs (e.g., this leaf falls), *they* have occurred. Nothing occurs or exists while waiting for its causes to occur. The entire series of causes "behind" the present condition or event is *over and done with*. We are not still waiting for any members of that series to come about.

Now a causal series cannot have occurred if there is no *first* member of that series. A causal series cannot be completed in one direction, toward the relevant effect, and not in the other. It is, after all, one and the same series. This means that there was a first event of this series. That first event had no cause or ground *within* the series of physical causation. That is not to say it had no cause at all, but it is to say that its cause must be something not itself a part of the series of physical causation. Thus, *a cause or source that is not a physical condition or event lies at the origin of the causal order that is the physical world*. The fall of the leaf or the current state of the physical universe as a whole has a source or cause that is not physical.

SOME HELP FROM FAMILIAR IMAGES

To follow arguments such as this makes great demands upon our mental concentration and thought habits. That is likely to prevent us from following out the line of reasoning to the conclusion to be drawn. We will then fail to achieve knowledge of that conclusion. To aid our comprehension, consider the following familiar image. You have a line of dominoes standing on end in such a way that if one is pushed over, it knocks over the next one in the direction it falls, and so on down the line. Now imagine a line of dominoes falling toward your right and a line of those already having fallen disappearing over the horizon to your left.

Someone suggests that the line to your left has no first member. They are saying that for every domino in the sequence to your left there is another fallen domino beyond it to your left, which made it fall. That is to say, the sequence of falling dominoes leading up to this one now falling right before you here is *unlimited*, infinite, with no first member. That amounts to the claim that there is no domino that falls without being knocked over by another domino falling upon it. But if there were no first domino to fall, not knocked over by another domino, there would be no last one before *this* one, to make this one fall, and so it would not fall. But it does fall. There is such a last one, so there is a first one, a first domino to fall.

If there were no first domino to fall, the sequence of falling dominoes to the left would be unlimited or infinite, and it would never "reach" the domino that, just having fallen, knocks over the one falling here and now in front of you. Viewed from the point of view of the progressively falling dominoes coming from the left—from the "other end," as it were—there would always be more dominoes to fall before reaching *this* one. (Is your head spinning? Go slowly.)

There are other ways of developing this same point in imagination. Suppose I told you that I have on my desk a photocopy for which there is no original, just an endless series of copies of copies? Would you believe it? Or that there is a stack of books somewhere without a bottom book. Or a chain hanging from links above it—only no topmost link. Note that these are all series of *dependencies* that are *completed*. (This book *is* supported here, that link *is* hanging there.) Note also that there is no reference to time or to human limitations in this argument. Or, Greg Jesson suggests, consider a fan running plugged into an extension cord, plugged into an extension cord, into an extension cord, with no "first "extension cord.

A PRELIMINARY SUMMARY

This completes the *demonstration of the existence of a nonphysical reality in addition to the physical universe,* where "physical" is understood in the standard way. To sum up, the dependent character of all physical states, together with the completeness of the series of dependencies underlying the existence of any given physical state, thing, or event, logically implies at least one self-existent, and therefore nonphysical, state of being or entity, a state of being or entity *radically different from* those that make up the physical or "natural" world. It is demonstrably absurd that there should be a self-sufficient physical universe, if by that we mean an all-inclusive totality of entities and events of the familiar or scientific physical variety. We could, like Spinoza, attempt to treat the universe itself as having an essentially different type of being from the physical, but then that would only be to concede our point about the existence of a nonphysical realm.

To avoid the conclusion to this line of reasoning, one might try to:

1. Deny that physical conditions and events have a beginning or a first such condition or event—that there is a "singularity," as the "big bang" is sometimes called; or,

2. Affirm that the "singularity" occurred with no prior existent, "out of nothing"; or,

3. Affirm that the physical world is, after all, not physical, or perhaps that it does not exist, that it is an illusion.

But none of these can be sustained as known truth, and the first and second are clearly false. Of course, philosophical debates rarely come to a satisfactory end for all parties concerned. This is partly because they dig so deeply into how we must think about our life and our world and have serious implications for how we are to live and act. Also, those debates are often absorbed in mere logical possibilities that have little bearing on life as serious claims to knowledge of reality.[11] However, there is a life side to the question we are here discussing: an issue of how one is to live responsibly, given what can be known to be true or, at a minimum, what is reasonable to accept and to act upon *as* true. In any area—say politics or personal relationships—one does not necessarily *have to know* what is in itself quite knowable. That is certainly true in matters concerning God. At least for now.

Our claim here is only that knowledge of the nonphysical source of the physical universe is possible to those who will invest *due diligence* concerning the matter. Many people actually do know that there is such a source. All of this is quite consistent with the fact that many people do not know it as well as the fact that many people who do know it also reject it—will not have it to be so—and refuse to acknowledge what they know to be the case. To know something, we recall, is *to represent it as it is on an appropriate basis of thought and experience.* To understand the basic character of the physical world is, we have pointed out, to be in a position to know that it has a nonphysical source, that is, a "Creator" of some nonphysical sort. But one way of *not* knowing what is quite knowable is to refuse to think matters out to the end—refuse to "follow the argument"—in a carefully attentive and thorough manner. And when people sense that something is coming around the logical corner that they *will* not to be so, they often just refuse to carefully follow the argument. It's as common as sin, and a large part of it too.

WHAT HAVE WE GAINED?

We should pause at this point to see what we have and have not gained. Very proper objections are sometimes directed at "cosmological arguments" because they overreach and try to draw more from the premises than the premises will validly support. For example, St. Thomas Aquinas gives his reasons for a "first mover, moved by no other." Very well. I think he got there. But then he adds, "And this everyone understands to be God." But wait a minute, we want to say. Certainly a first mover is a long way from the God *he* is talking about and that we are interested in here, the "God and Father of our Lord Jesus Christ." So there is obviously a great deal of work yet to do, and it is not certain that it can be done. We have to build carefully on what we really have achieved if we are to advance in knowledge of the God indicated in the opening paragraphs of this chapter.

But on the other hand, we *have* achieved a great deal, and it opens the way for us to go forward. Those who reject the existence of God or the possibility of knowledge of him now have a haunted universe on their hands. It is haunted by unnerving actualities and accompanying possibilities. The above argument shows conclusively that *there is something more than the physical or "natural" universe, something of very impressive proportions.* It is something quite different from the physical world in character and something from which the physical derives its existence and nature. If this is established, it is not clear that there is much point to blanket atheism, though there still could be objections to this or that particular *kind* of "god." Atheism in the contemporary world draws most of its motivation from a desire to *tame* or to *naturalize* reality. All hope for that is now lost, and it looks like the "natural" realm is also ripe for invasion by something that is not it. Religion as a historical reality in human life as well as certain kinds of gods can still be attacked by atheists—often well deserved. But there is an obvious sense in which atheists can never again feel at ease in a universe that supplements the physical realm in the way required by the argument we have just gone through.

KNOWLEDGE OF THIS "SOMETHING MORE"

Proceeding very carefully, can we know anything more about this "Creator" other than that it is and that it is not physical? I think we can.

First of all, we know that this "source" must be of great power to have produced the physical universe. Exactly how big we cannot know, but it must be quite large. If we are to take seriously the equation $e = mc^2$, the source of the physical world must involve enough e (energy) to translate into the m (mass) of the physical universe. That is a lot of energy. This equation is not a statement about how much energy exists, but about the amount of energy in a given amount of physical substance. From the human point of view we have mass in various forms around us, and we want to get the energy out of it. That is the human quest: power and more power. We know something about energy in relation to mass, but not about how much energy exists or all the forms it might take apart from matter. Consciousness or the mental, obviously, does "work," brings about change, so it too must be a form of energy. But our understanding of exactly what consciousness is is very small, to put it mildly; even more so with respect to a "divine consciousness."

Second, the nonphysical source of the physical world is not a *merely* causal system. We can know that. If it were, then the causal sequence of the physical world would not terminate at it, but would continue on, only now in a nonphysical or "spiritual" medium. But that is ruled out by the impossibility of an infinite causal series being completed at the point where the leaf falls, and so forth. The source of the physical world must have the capacity to *initiate* causal sequences while being itself not *caused* to act. This capacity in human life is known as *will*, and its exercise is known as *choice*. In choosing, we human beings initiate causal sequences—tipping over the first domino, for example—without being simply caused or forced to do so. The "first mover" of the physical world must have the capacity of will, then, or something very like it, if the causal series behind the physical universe and events in it is, as we have seen, not to be infinite.

Third, we can also know that the creator must *think,* must have the power of thought and must exercise that power in the choices it makes. Choice is consciously selective and directional. It attends not only to what it does and the results of that, but to possibilities of what it might do. This is the nature of intellect. The idea of blind will, which philosophers sometimes have toyed with, is simply a contradiction of terms if one means willing without conscious selectivity or direction. Of course, many of our actions, possibly most, do not actually involve choice, but only impulse or habit. And there are many *forces* other than will and choice, mostly blind. Causation itself is "blind," though it is directional, always producing not just any effect, but a specific one. Still, choice as the outcome of deliberation between alternatives is never blind.

THE "DESIGN" ARGUMENT

Under this third point an additional point about the intellect of the "source" comes into play. The *order* that is glaringly present in the physical world has led many thoughtful people to conclude that the source of that order must involve intellect, and a very high degree of intellect. The quotations from Epictetus and Hume given above illustrate that conclusion, as does the recent "conversion" of Professor Antony Flew from a lifetime of aggressive atheism to a deistic brand of theism. But what is the line of reasoning that leads to this conclusion? Is it logically cogent?

The basic premise here is suggested by Epictetus's statement. We human beings have many, many experiences of ordered wholes and processes emerging from the thoughts and choices of human beings. One known source of some order—in birthday cakes and airplanes, for example—is human thought and action.

No doubt about that. In these cases, of course, the "thought" or "designing" does not result in order emerging from "nothing," but out of preexisting materials with a nature and order of their own. Nevertheless, the obvious role of intellect in the production of some order is a fact with which most human beings are thoroughly familiar.

We also know that *some* order arises from other ordered things without the direct intervention of intellect in the manner of birthday cakes and airplanes. Puppies come from dogs and dogs from puppies; apples come from apple trees and the trees from apple seeds, in cooperation with the surrounding orders of sunshine, soil, and water. The question arises: Could the order that we find in the natural world, which we know not to have arisen through *human* intellect and action, have come about *without the intervention of any intellect at all?*

So far as our experience goes, to say the least, the emergence of ordered physical things or processes—puppies, apples, erosion (the Grand Canyon), tide pools—always depends upon prior ordered beings and processes. But this, we have already seen on other grounds, must eventuate in something that is not a physical reality. *That* "something," we have further seen, must involve something very like human will (choice) and thought. Since we know that in a limited way—the human way—thought does inject order into existence, it seems obvious that the will and intellect that are the source of the physical world must inject into the physical world at large the order that we find there. Possibly some order that is not from the human intellect even has the capacity to generate further order. (The British philosopher William Paley long ago imagined a watch that could make other watches.) The origin of "natural" orders in a nonhuman intellect is, at least, the "best explanation" we have of the radical origin of natural order, of the laws and facts that make up the field of nature.

Are there any alternatives to this? None that seem remotely plausible. The idea that physical order could arise from *nothing*—

that there might have been nothing, physical or otherwise, and then a physical order of things—is already refuted by the truth that nothing physical arises from nothing. We have already examined this matter. But popular imagination sometimes runs wild on this point. The editors of the Time-Life book *Cosmos* gravely remark that "no one can say with certainty why the universe popped out of the void."[12] They, along with many sober cosmologists who ponder this question, seem oblivious to the fact that in the nature of the case there can be no *why* for its "popping out," since it is precisely the *void*, the "empty," out of which it is supposed to pop. There is nothing to be uncertain about.

WHAT ABOUT EVOLUTION?

Currently many people try to invoke evolution as a completely general answer to the question of the source of order in the physical world. But once you understand what evolution is, you immediately see that there are severe limitations on its explanation of the emergence of ordered things. In particular, evolution *presupposes* an elaborate order or "design" in things *before* it can occur. We briefly mentioned this above. Evolution presupposes life and an arrangement to secure all of propagation, inheritance, and modification of inheritance, along with an environment that determines which organisms will survive and propagate and which will not. This elaborate arrangement clearly cannot be produced or accounted for by evolution itself, because it is a condition of evolution occurring at all.

Moreover, evolution is but one process among many within the physical world. It is an elaborate order or "design" in its own right, and *its* existence is not the result of evolution, since nothing is the result of itself. Evolution is not a cosmic absolute, a self-sufficient and self-explanatory being that explains all else. In the larger physical scheme, in fact, it explains very little and would not be missed in a universe just like ours in all other respects, but without living things. Evolution itself certainly did not evolve into being.

Because of the confused state of the public mind with reference to evolution, the following points deserve reemphasis. The origin of physical order in general cannot be explained by evolution. Evolution itself is an "order" that requires explanation if any order does, and it presupposes, as we have just seen, a vast scale of order and existence within which alone it can occur. Whether evolution occurs with regard to plant and animal species (which was Darwin's concern), that has no serious implications at all, taken by itself, for the existence of God. Given the line of argument in this chapter, evolution would itself count in favor of the existence of God, as indeed many have insisted.

FINAL SUMMARY OF RESULTS

So now let us summarize our conclusions again. There exists a very great nonphysical being that is the source of the physical universe. This we now know to be the case if we have followed the argument. This being has capacities very like what we know in human beings as will and intellect. We recall David Hume's words that "the cause or causes of order in the universe probably bear some remote analogy to human intelligence." Again: "The whole frame of nature bespeaks an intelligent author; and no rational enquirer can, after serious reflection, suspend his belief a moment with regard to the primary principles of genuine Theism and Religion." Hume was, we acknowledge, talking about "rational belief" and not knowledge. But the reasons that held him back from *knowledge* of reality, leaving only what he called "rational belief" as an option, are highly dubious, to say the least, and not a burden any rational person must carry. The argument we have presented in this chapter is simple and straightforward, and its elements will bear up under any sincere scrutiny that does not lose itself in a maze of empty logical possibilities or imagings.

Some still may say that this does not give us the loving Father God of whom Jesus spoke, who came among humanity in the person of his Son and went through death and resurrection with him and with us. That is true, but we have not yet come to the end of the story. Our argument thus far *does* give us a magnificent "Creator," though not yet a personal presence in human history and in individual lives—not a perfectly good God of love. However, we say once again, *do not underestimate the importance of what we have gained*. Now the entire cognitive landscape has been changed, and with it real *possibilities* of knowledge of such a personal presence in the world and of a spiritual life for human beings in union with God the Creator—in short, knowledge of what the Apostles' Creed states. With this in mind we turn to consider the possibility of knowledge of the "miraculous," of the intervention of God the Creator in the affairs of human beings.

FOR DISCUSSION

1. How is knowledge of God (his existence and nature) related to knowledge of Christ?

2. What are some important details in the biblical vision of God? What is he like?

3. Does the apostle Paul hold that human beings have, or *could* have, adequate knowledge of God? Why have they lost it? What is the basis of such knowledge?

4. Does the physical universe have a beginning? Did it not exist, and then exist?

5. How is a beginning of the physical universe inconsistent with the "*causal closure* of physical reality"? (A beginning implies that the physical universe is "open.")

6. "I have in my office a copy for which there is no original." Can this be?

7. What exactly is gained by the argument for God from the existence of the physical world? Does it take us "all the way"? Why or why not?

8. Can we know anything more about the "creator" of the physical world than that it exists and that it is *not* something physical? Perhaps that it is a personal being or personlike?

9. Is the presence of amazing order in the physical world an *additional* point in favor of a personal creator?

10. Would *biological* evolution, if it were true, affect the argument for a personal creator? How would it do so? (It would be, after all, but one more case of intricate order, and it would have to be accounted for.)

11. "Now the entire cognitive landscape has been changed" (last paragraph of this chapter). What does this mean?

The Miraculous, and Christ's Presence in Our World

Why is it thought incredible by any of you that God raises the dead?

PAUL, ACTS 26:8

WE HAVE NOW found a firm basis for *knowing* that there is a vast nonphysical being underlying—perhaps also interpenetrating—the reality of the physical universe. We have pointed out that, although this is a knowable fact, no one *has* to know it. There are many people who do not know it. Either through neglect or resolve, they can refuse to seek out or attend to the considerations that would naturally lead to their knowing that there is a reality other than the physical world, one of magnificent proportions and intriguing character. The fact that some or many people do not know this or even deny it has of itself no bearing whatsoever upon whether it is knowable or whether some or many others do in fact know it.

At this point in our study we are somewhat limited as to what we can justifiably claim to know of the *character* of this great reality, but we do have some promising thoughts about it.

First of all, we know, with C. S. Lewis, that "what is behind the [physical] universe is more like a mind than it is like anything else we know."[1] And we recall once again the words of David Hume—certainly no friend to knowledge of God: "The whole frame of nature bespeaks an intelligent author; and no rational enquirer can, after serious reflection, suspend his belief a moment with regard to the primary principles of genuine Theism and Religion."

But if followers of Jesus Christ are to claim that what *they* believe is, in large or significant measure, something that can also be known, then knowing, or the possibility of it, must reach far beyond anything established to this point. In the Apostles' Creed immediately after "I believe in God, the Father Almighty" come the words "and in Jesus Christ, his only Son, our Lord," followed in turn by a list of *particular events and conditions* that clearly require the intervention of God in the course of physical nature as well as his active presence on an ongoing basis with those who are Jesus's disciples or students.

THE HALF-BELIEVERS: DEISM

It is, of course, with reference to just such interventions and presence that Hume and others, such as (famously) Thomas Jefferson and Thomas Paine in the American context, along with a great deal of what is now called "liberal" Christianity, part company with "mere Christianity." For reasons to which we now turn, intervention into human affairs through events that lie outside the normal course of nature has been rejected by many people who nevertheless say they believe in the "laws of nature and nature's God." The term that has for centuries been applied to those who believe in "God, but no more" and that is accepted enthusiastically by them today is "deists." "Deist" and "deism" are words that emerged into English usage in the course of philosophical controversies in Europe during the seventeenth century. Those controversies and the accompanying terminology continue to be influential today.

"Deist" derives from the Latin term for "God," and "theist" from the Greek term for "God." Deists and theists both believe in the existence of a personal God. The deist, Immanuel Kant said, believes in a God, but theists believe in a *living* God, an *acting* God, such as is seen in the familiar biblical stories, while deists do not. So with regard to the intervention and presence of God in human life, deists believe much as atheists do—except old-fashioned deists often held the belief that God has a moral claim upon human lives and even that "in the end" they would stand before his judgment. In practical terms, however, contemporary deists are indistinguishable from atheists. The often rather intense moral interest of earlier deists[2] has now vanished.

There can be little doubt about the primary impulse behind deism, which, again, it shares with much to be found in atheism and in many theologically liberal writers today. That is resistance to the claims of human beings to be able to speak and act for God and with God. Of course, such claims are central to biblical religion as well as to most of Christian history and to "mere Christianity." But it naturally calls forth resistance, because it seems to single out people in that tradition as having a "special place" with God and therefore a special authority among human beings.

Many people past and present have found this to be ominous or at least unwelcome. It naturally leads to resentment, anger, and rejection on the part of those "left out" or of those who claim a knowledge of God with a different content. Thus the earliest opponents of Christianity in the Roman world, such as Celsus, Porphyry, and Julian, responded to Christian claims of special actions by God with an objection that seems curiously contemporary. They said that Jesus himself was really a mere human whose disciples projected upon him the imaginary status of a divine being and thought up miraculous events or conditions—such as his claims to be divine, his various miracles, and especially his resurrection—to support their projection.

Faithful to this approach is a modern definition of deism from the contemporary World Union of Deists: "Deism is the recognition of a universal creative force greater than that demonstrated by humankind, supported by personal observation of laws and designs in nature and the universe, perpetuated and validated by the innate ability of human reason coupled with the rejection of claims made by individuals and organized religions of having received special divine revelation." Many people of high standing in the field of New Testament scholarship today are essentially deistic or atheistic in their views, and they accordingly try to treat the central teachings of Christianity as human constructions requiring no events of miraculous intervention in human affairs to account for Christian history. This is no secret.

WHY NOT DIVINE INTERVENTIONS?

It appears to some to be a strong argument against God's engagement with his creation, and with human life in particular, that much chaos, harm, and foolishness has been brought on by people claiming unique access to God. The religious wars of Europe were in large part due to claims people made to special standings and dealings with God. No doubt such claims lie behind all too much foolishness and injury by individuals in ordinary life. "Enthusiasm" and "superstition" were terms widely used to condemn such people in the past. To curb the "madness" of such people, much effort was put into the denial of the possibility of miracles during the seventeenth and eighteenth centuries. If miracles are not possible, such people are in error and have no just claim upon anyone's allegiance. They can be disregarded or shut down if they prove too troublesome.

But another line of thinking that resisted the possibility of divine intervention—we shall hereafter simply speak of "miracles"—was tied to how arguments *for* the existence of God were often presented around the seventeenth century. This was a period when the majestic order of the solar system and material universe was increasingly understood and taken as an indication of a majestic Creator. In fact it was taken to indicate a Creator so majestic, many presumed, that to think he had to come along later and "tinker" with his work was something of an insult to his dignity. He was thought of as so grand and self-sufficient that any idea that he might enjoy or express himself though continued creative interaction with his creatures could only be seen as too humanlike to deserve serious consideration. The divine majesty was surely above all of that! That he would actually "show up" to communicate with and act with human beings was out of the question. He would not be seen in such company!

Religion as a historical human practice was therefore not of divine origin, and its developments and activities had to be of an entirely human origin.[3] "Religious studies" as now practiced in our academies is strictly keyed to this curiously secular understanding of religion. You might well think that a secular understanding of religion would amount to simply changing the subject. And arguably it has amounted to that. So much effort has been invested by modern and contemporary thinkers in a secular interpretation of religion that religion can now be studied with no reference to God at all. This suits the deistic temperament as well as a strictly secular view of human life, but simply omits religion as would be understood by almost everyone who has practiced it.

A "SECULAR" BIBLE?

One very significant aspect of this amazing approach to religion is seen in what has come to be regarded in academic circles as the only intellectually responsible approach to the Bible. That approach sees the Bible merely as one historical artifact among others, to be understood in strictly human terms. Read in a fairly straightforward way, but with all due scholarly care, the Old Testament, for example, might easily appear as "a magnificent demonstration of the immense and, on natural principles, inexplicable difference between the religion of this obscure people [the Jews] and every other."[4] That is, the Jewish religion might appear as a work of divine intervention on behalf of the Jews and even in the production of the very text of the Old Testament. The Bible itself might be regarded as a supernatural work of God. To a vast body of sane and capable scholars it had so appeared in the past. However, if from the very outset any "divine intervention" into human affairs must be ruled out, such a supernatural presence is not permitted as an outcome and any nonhuman presence or activity must therefore be disallowed in understanding what the biblical text is, how it came to be, and in what it says.[5]

This means that any obvious supernatural component in what the Bible plainly does say—that, for example, Moses parted the Red Sea or that Jesus resumed a bodily existence some days after his death—has to be explained in some way other than as a statement of fact. Also, the Bible's very existence and nature must be understood without any reference to the action of God in human affairs to produce it and preserve it.

Now, if the Bible and its contents were to be taken as the *only* evidence for the existence of God—if we had no independent evidence of God's existence apart from the Bible and its stories and statements—then one might see why the Bible should be approached with such a secularist mind-set. We should not then allow as an assumption in reading it what (the action of God) was supposed to be proven only by reading it. Of course. But the governing assumption of the secularist approach to the Bible and to Jewish and Christian traditions—namely, that there is no God, or that if there is, he has nothing to do with the Bible or with the traditions or events cited in it—is an assumption totally without foundation in fact or in plausible theory. No one has proven it or rendered it plausible. The fields of biblical studies thus submitted themselves to a priori and groundless assumptions that supernatural reality has nothing to do with the subject matters of those fields. Those fields then had to "account" for everything they dealt with on secular—deistic, if not atheistic—assumptions.

BUT IS REALITY SECULAR?

The result of our previous chapter indicates a substantial basis for questioning the truth of those assumptions. Since there is such a vast nonphysical (spiritual) reality, as we have discovered, secularism itself, as a view of reality and knowledge, cannot stand as an unquestioned truth, to say the very least, or as something that without question can govern our approach to any subject matter, much less that of religion and the Bible.

George Bernard Shaw, a clever but shallow thinker, used to say that the phrase "Catholic university" was an oxymoron, a self-contradictory expression. What he meant was that, if you are a Catholic, you are committed to views that could not be critically examined by you and made to stand the test of free inquiry as to truth and reason. That is what a university is supposed to do to all views. But if that was true of the Catholic universities he had in mind, it certainly is true of the universities that proudly describe themselves as "secular" today.[6]

Is reality secular? Is adequate knowledge secular? And is that something that has been established as a fact by thorough and unbiased inquiry? Is that something that today's "secular" universities thoroughly and freely discuss in a disciplined way? Certainly not! Nowhere does that happen. And any suggestion that it *should* happen would not be treated as a serious intellectual proposal—if it were considered at all.

It is now *simply assumed* that every field of knowledge or practice is perfectly complete without any reference to God as real and relevant, and all the more so without any knowledge of God and his activities. It may be *logically* possible that this assumption is true. But *is* it true, and is there reason to think that it is true? Could there be knowledge on *that* point, knowledge that could be taught as such before the objectively critical mind? Published in peer-review professional journals? It certainly hasn't been done, nor is it on the horizon.

So we are left with two reasons given for ruling out the intervention of God—miracles, for short—in human affairs. One is that claims to divine intervention lead to such foolishness and harmfulness that all such claims should be rejected out of hand. The second is the "deistic" argument that it is, somehow, beneath God's dignity to interact with human beings or with the universe he has, it is granted, created. Neither of these "reasons" has much in favor of it when carefully considered. God's "dignity," as conceived of by deists, actually seems far too much like the "dignity" of human beings filled with their own self-importance. Anyway, how could deists, on their premises, know that much about God's character and personality?

On the other hand, although all sorts of foolish and harmful things are no doubt done by those who claim to be guided or touched by God, that is no reason to think God had anything to do with those things or to think, by contrast, that those who, with exactly similar claims, do extraordinarily good and wise things are *not* guided and empowered by God. One would think that foolishness and evil have by now been proven to flourish in utter disconnection from religious claims to sponsorship by God. They are thoroughly human and in no need of specifically religious claims, though they are frequently accompanied by them. As we have seen above, some have sought to close down even human claims to know what is *morally* good and right to help eliminate human foolishness and harm. There surely has to be a better way.

ARE MIRACLES JUST IMPOSSIBLE?

Perhaps the line of reasoning now most widely accepted against the occurrence of those miraculous events that lie at the heart of "mere Christianity" simply alleges the *impossibility* of any such events. Is this a solid line of thought? It says that there are *natural laws,* and that these require that regularities in events of the physical realm are unbreakable, impossible to interrupt. The miraculous intervention of God into human affairs would mean a setting aside of such regularities. Therefore it does not happen. Just that simple. So the basic teachings of historic Christianity *cannot* be true, and therefore cannot be known to be true. There can be no knowledge of them. A secular account of religion in all its forms must, accordingly, be correct.

We note two things to begin our discussion of this position. First, there are indeed general regularities in physical events, and these are rarely if ever interrupted. The inception of new life in the human female's womb regularly requires the injection of sperm from a human male, dead people regularly stay dead, and on a regular basis water refuses to turn into wine even when spoken to. Second, however, unusual events do occur. Sometimes we are, perhaps much later, able to explain why they occur—"The Connecticut Yankee in King Arthur's Court" type cases, among others—and when we are able to do so it is always found that some other "law" comes into play. For example, iron regularly sinks when placed in water. Yes, but then we find that if it is hollowed out or given a certain shape, it does not sink. A law of "displacement" comes into play. Or we know that people regularly die of certain diseases or die at a certain rate. But then we find that injecting them with certain substances prevents their death. This means that common regularities in nature all depend upon certain conditions that lie deeper in reality, and that if those conditions are modified, then the regularities are interrupted. That is a quite general truth we can regard as established from known cases.

NATURE'S REGULARITIES ARE ALL CONDITIONED

That raises the question of the *ultimate* conditions upon which the regularities of nature depend. These ultimate conditions, as we have already seen, lie outside of physical nature itself in the nonphysical source of the physical universe or "nature." The very laws of nature and the "regularities" corresponding to them depend upon whatever is the source of nature. That the laws of nature are laws of nature is not something explainable by the laws of nature themselves, but only by the source of those laws, whatever it is. It is not a law of nature that there be laws of nature, nor that there be the ones we actually have.

Now, we do have some idea of how natural regularities might be interrupted from observing human practices of intervening in natural processes. This we constantly do in various ways. We interrupt the decay of food, for example, by refrigerating it, the withering and death of a plant by watering it. Within limits, with our limited powers, we know how to do such things across a broad range of natural regularities. Our thoughts, feelings, and choices intervene in the course of otherwise inevitable events.

Since, as we now know, the ultimate conditions of the physical universe with its laws lie in a nonphysical being of great proportions, it is not unreasonable to think that that being *could* modify the conditions of well-known regularities in such a way as to produce the miraculous events central to the Christian tradition and the Christian life. There is then no question of the *possibility* of interventions in the course of nature, in whatever degree or form. The physical universe is not a closed system. Miracles are possible simply because of that fact.

HUME AND LEWIS ON MIRACLES

Taking David Hume's famous and influential definition of "miracle" as a violation of natural law or the interruption of one of nature's regularities, C. S. Lewis pointed out that, in Hume's own views, the only reason to believe that there are natural laws or that nature is "uniform" is the existence of a rational creator who sees to it that nature *is* uniform. If nature is uniform then, in this view, it is so on the same basis as miracles might occur, namely, the purposes of the creator.

Independently of Hume, however, we can now say, on the basis of our inquiries here, that there is *something* other than nature that accounts for nature and the regularities of nature. The laws of nature are "his" or "its" arrangements. And if they are, then he or it *can* change the conditions and manners of those arrangements to allow for or to bring about events that are totally out of character for nature "on its own." Nature is, simply, not on its own. But then both the laws of nature and the change of their higher-level conditions—along with any resultant miraculous event and its "natural" consequences—are a part of a larger system of reality including both nature and the special purposes of God.[7]

All of this being so, no one can with good reason reject the miraculous central teachings of Christian tradition and life on the grounds that it is *impossible* for such events to occur among human beings. To repeat the basic points, physical reality is not a causally "closed" system. Its very coming into existence, with or without God, is by itself sufficient to show that it is not a closed system, and that the often alleged "causal closure of the physical" is just false. Since it *is* false, the *possibility* of genuinely miraculous interventions into human life is secured. And if it is possible that the entire physical world "came from nothing," surely miraculous events could do the same.

POSSIBLE, BUT ARE MIRACLES EVER ACTUAL?

But even so, whether any miracles actually have occurred and whether given events that did occur were miracles are additional issues. And they are ones we need to be very careful about. Claims to involvement with miraculous events, even when hardly plausible, do give people great power and influence in human affairs. Often great harm *is* done by them. That is why established religious bodies, such as the Catholic church, often have elaborate procedures for testing events presented as miracles to see if they really are. Deists and their liberal counterparts were right to be concerned about the effects of claims to God's interventions, though they were wrong in the way they tried to respond to the problem. Well-meaning Christians and people from other religions have done dangerous and foolish things in the name of miracles, misleading themselves and harming others. But how can we *know* that a miraculous event has actually occurred or that a particular event we know to have occurred was actually a miracle—a genuine manifestation of extranatural power? A "miracle" might be something truly spectacular or a simple answer to prayer.

TESTIMONY AND MIRACLES

To know that miraculous events have actually occurred in this or that situation, which would be necessary in order to *know* the truth of essential Christian beliefs, obviously rests upon some sort of evidence. The witness or testimony of individuals to events in question would be important in this connection. That is not just because events central to religious traditions—the events of the Exodus of the Jews from Egypt, for example, or those in the New Testament involving Jesus Christ—occurred long ago and the written and institutional testimonies to them are the major, if not the only, source of information about them. Rather, corroborating experience is useful in determining the meaning of observable events. If a highly unusual event occurs right before your eyes—the appearance of a UFO, for example—you will be uncertain about what happened and about what you actually saw.

If others are standing by in such a situation, you will most likely exclaim, "Did you see that?" Their "testimony" in response to your question will be important in settling your mind about what exactly it was that you saw, but even that may not be definitive.

This necessity, among other things, exposes the fallacy of those who say they *would* believe if God would just "do something"—usually something bizarre. Norwood Hanson, for example, says he will believe in God if

> on next Tuesday morning, just after our breakfast, all of us in this one world are knocked to our knees by a percussive and ear-shattering thunderclap. Snow swirls; leaves drop from trees; the earth heaves and buckles; buildings topple and towers tumble; the sky is ablaze with an eerie, silvery light. Just then, as all the people of this world look up, the heavens open—the clouds pull apart—revealing an unbelievably immense and radiant Zeus-like figure, towering up above us like a hundred Everests. He frowns darkly as lightning plays across the features of his Michaelangeloid face. He then points down—*at me!*—and exclaims, for every man, woman and child to hear: "I have had quite enough of your too-clever logic-chopping and word-watching in matters of theology. Be assured, N. R. Hanson, that I do most certainly exist."[8]

But would he "believe"? Almost certainly he would not. And if he did, he would not be believing in *God*. That thing that appeared, whatever it was, was not God, just something very big. Would he worship it? Would he think that *that* was the creator of the physical universe? Would he think it was holy? Or just amazing and scary? He would perhaps visit a psychiatrist, and then perhaps he would begin to think about what could be accomplished by "special effects." He would mull over a few episodes of *Star Trek*. Or he might seek out someone from a relevant tradition on such events. (Is there one? Perhaps that of the Olympian "deities" of ancient Greece?) The interpretation of unusual events requires some sort of community and traditional framework within which they might make sense, if they are to make sense at all. The credibility of a miraculous event depends upon a long tradition of events and interpretations. Believing it is not something you just up and *do* all by yourself.

Hanson builds witnesses into his imaginary event. But they would have no better idea of what they were looking at than he did. And if, as David Hume held, the main—possibly the only—evidence for a miracle is the testimony of witnesses, then, eventually, there is no "hard" evidence for the miracles to which they testify. Witnesses at some point must encounter facts and make sense of them. Otherwise the evidence they have for any miracle to which they testify could only be the testimony of others—or no evidence at all. One suspects from other comments that this may have been Hume's intent.[9] But just as experience of a "miraculous" event will make sense only in the context of other witnesses and a tradition in which they stand, so "testimony" works only if at some point it transcends itself and finds corroboration in the experience of events in the world. Otherwise it is *only* "hearsay."

CAUSAL CONSEQUENCES OF THE EVENT

The testimony of witnesses and direct perception of events are essential to knowledge of miracles, but evidence for the occurrence of a miraculous event is also to be derived from its consequences. Any event that occurs, miraculous or not, becomes a part of the reality (natural or supernatural) that proceeds from it. In recent years a project has been undertaken to discover the residues of the Egyptian army that, according to the story in the book of Exodus, was swallowed up when the Red Sea closed over it as it pursued the Israelites. If a suitable array of physical objects, in an appropriate condition, were to be discovered at the bottom of the Red Sea, that would amount to serious evidence of a miraculous event. Present facts, under certain circumstances, indicate past realities. In this case an empirical hypothesis was formulated on the basis of an old story, and it was tested with (we can imagine) a result strongly confirming the hypothesis drawn from the miracle story. How strong the confirmation was would of course depend on the details. Similarly for the project of finding something like Noah's ark on Mt. Ararat in Turkey, which has been occasionally attempted. And so forth. "Miraculous" events leave the "testimony" of real and distinctive consequences behind them, just like all other events.

The occurrence of the miraculous event eventually must leave evidence beyond testimony from past or present witnesses. On the other hand, whether it was a genuine act of God rather than merely the product of unknown "natural" processes is not something that is strictly *observed* by anyone. That is a conclusion to be reached on the basis of one's understanding of what is "natural" and what is not. The importance of the spectacular cases—fire from heaven in response to human speaking, the raising of the dead, and so forth—lies in the fact that few are prepared to question their supernatural causation, though that has been tried. And to elicit such events by human speaking (to God in prayer or directly to the situation and circumstances involved) certainly does not fall within the range of natural causation. If they happen, they are pretty certainly miracles. In their case, opponents of miracles are, realistically, limited to denying they happened at all.

THE PATTERN OF INQUIRY

In any case, the investigation of whether a miraculous event has occurred in a given case would be conducted along familiar lines of inquiry. One begins with the assumption that the event in question occurred—the unlikely defeat of the Spanish Armada, the Exodus of the Israelites from Egypt, the resurrection of Jesus from the dead—and then one estimates the probability of it occurring "within" the boundaries of "natural" regularities. If that is *highly* improbable, then we have good evidence that it is a miracle and that a miracle actually occurred. Skeptics will at that point want to go back and question whether the event actually occurred. That is all well and good. In pursuing knowledge no stone is to be left unturned. If the event did not occur, then of course it was no miracle. So, once again, familiar lines of inquiry are to be followed with thoroughness and honesty. Christians ask for no special treatment, but only fair and thorough inquiry.

All of this is not to say it is somehow wrong or illegitimate for people to believe in the miraculous events chronicled in the Bible or Christian history without doing all of the work that goes into a firsthand knowing of them to be real. We do know many things in life on the basis of what others know. Obviously, *most* people who do believe in miracles will not be able, or if able, not willing, to do such work. But it makes a great deal of difference to them and to others *whether those events actually happened* and whether *someone* knows they did. This is the point at issue in this book, where we are dealing with the *cultural calamity of displacing the central points of Christian knowledge into the domain of mere "faith," sentiment, traditional ritual, or power.* If this displacement is correct, then it is, in some important sense, improper to believe that the central events of the Christian tradition actually happened. And it would be wrong to speak or teach them with the aim of eliciting belief in them on the basis of knowledge of reality.

THE RESURRECTION OF CHRIST

There is no doubt that the event most central to the Christian tradition after the existence of God is the resurrection of Jesus Christ. It does not stand alone, of course, but when viewed in the human context in which the original disciples of Jesus lived, everything else comes together around it. The Christian story is a story of human redemption from sin and from the power of evil. It is a story of the power of Jesus to overcome evil without engaging in it—of how he lives beyond all that evil can do against him or us. He has to be victorious in this battle. His status as Redeemer is not compatible with a failure to overcome death and to do so in a way that can be shared with those bodily beings we call "human." Thus the apostle Paul bluntly says, "If Christ has not been raised, . . . you are still in your sins" (1 Cor. 15:17). So now let us ask: Could one know that Jesus Christ actually rose from the dead and continued to exist after his death in bodily presence and interaction from time to time with his precrucifixion friends? If one can know it, then it actually happened.

The basic issue here is whether events subsequent to what is claimed as the resurrection of Christ could have been what they are if it hadn't actually happened. There is little doubt that if they happened, they were not natural events. So let us try to get a grip on the essentials of what it means to say that Christ arose from the dead, that is, to say that he continued to exist in a bodily form after his death by crucifixion. Those essentials include:

1. That he interacted with his friends by visible presence and by communications of the usual human sort.

2. That he had a body with many of the usual human dimensions as well as with some very unusual traits. It was a "glorious" body, according to observers, and had some amazing abilities with reference to the physical world. This provided a transition to the third essential:

3. That he continued to be active in this world among his contemporaries in various ways, and beyond them up to the present time, being available to those who seek him and who stand for and with him now.

Do events subsequent to Christ's death indicate that these "essentials" actually occurred? That would indicate that he existed well after his death, and for some time at least in a bodily form that permitted familiar interactions with ordinary human beings. The evidence in favor of these essentials is mainly the *transformation* of his followers from a small group of highly unqualified and socially marginalized individuals, disgraced and hunted by the authorities, into *a force for moral and social regeneration* that, within a few generations, was present throughout the Roman Empire and, within a few centuries, had become the dominant form of religion in it.[10] All of this came about without any special advantage other than the words they spoke and the life they lived, without any use of force and even against strong and often deadly opposition.

Can we know that Christ arose from the dead? Yes, if we will but "do the math." That he arose is the only plausible explanation for what happened after his death and what still exists today as a consequence. The established mental habit of many people today is to say with no thought, no hesitation, that he did not arise. There are numerous causes of this. For one thing, to many people this is a "religious" question, and *therefore* it automatically falls outside the domain of facts and knowledge. We have earlier addressed the error in such an attitude. Many such people are simply bored with a question they take to be irrelevant to real life anyway and don't want to be bothered with it. Also, allowing that it might be known that Christ arose is to concede that it actually happened, and that puts an entirely different light on individual life and human destiny.[11]

Suddenly reality is no longer safely secular. The apostle Paul's statement to the Athenians—that God "has fixed a day on which he will have the world judged in righteousness by a man whom he has appointed, and of this he has given assurance to all by raising him from the dead" (Acts 17:31)—would then be frighteningly plausible. Something is going on here that secularists had not counted on. It looks as if we are all going to be held responsible to God for what we do and who we have become. Suddenly the whole educational outlook of "modern" humanity is called into question and may be radically inadequate to reality. You can see why our system of "education" would use every available device to evade knowledge of the resurrection of Christ.

Some time ago Wolfhart Pannenberg discussed the work of Frank Tipler, who gives what he takes to be physical reasons for the eschatological raising of the dead—resurrection at the end of history—but rejects the resurrection of Jesus. He rejects it for what he calls "historical reasons." Pannenberg rightly asks why, given the immanence of the transcendent God, what is eschatologically final could not also be present in the midst of history. He points out that "many exegetes are in agreement that the core of the Christian Easter traditions is not a matter of legends, and if the content of what was reported were not so unusual, there would be no doubt of its historicity. The stumbling block is the supposed physical impossibility, and because of that, we have alternative reconstructions of the tradition that are historically more improbable than the central assertions of the Christian tradition."[12] We have here shown that miracles, including the resurrection of Christ, are not a physical impossibility. But socially driven prejudice, especially in fields of scholarship, blinds even some of those who understand the inherent openness of physical reality to transcendent power.

Although there is intense resistance in the secular mind to the actuality of Christ's resurrection—a resistance that stands over that mind in judgment—the facts of the case are recalcitrant. They have been examined again and again by Christians and others in the modern period from William Paley to William Lane Craig.[13] After going over all of the various ways of thinking about the various aspects of the resurrection stories, Anglican theologian N. T. Wright concludes that fair and thorough historians must say that there really was a tomb where the dead body of Jesus was placed, but then there was a tomb with no body in it, and there really were meetings between Jesus and his earliest friends. How, he asks, are these two facts to be explained? And he replies:

> The easiest explanation by far is that these things happened because Jesus really was raised from the dead, and the disciples really did meet him, even though his body was renewed and transformed so that now it seemed to be able to live in two dimensions at once. (That, indeed, is perhaps the best way to understand the phenomena: Jesus was now living in God's dimension and ours, or, if you like, heaven and earth, simultaneously.) . . . The resurrection of Jesus does in fact provide a *sufficient* explanation for the empty tomb and the meetings with Jesus. Having examined all the other possible hypotheses I've read about anywhere in the literature, I think it's also a *necessary* explanation.[14]

The established *possibility* of resurrection, resting upon the openness of the physical universe to a nonphysical source or creator of it all, opens the door to consider fairly the evidence that strongly favors the resurrection of Christ as an actual event and favors his continued presence in this world. So the factuality of a major miracle in this world *can be known* by those who would like to know and who are willing to give adequate consideration to the available evidence. Perhaps the main responsibility for knowing it lies upon those who believe it. A reasonable next step would be openness to God's intervention in other contexts and, especially, in the events of their own lives today. Thus they could come to know the reality of a "spiritual life" for ordinary human beings (see the next chapter).

A Christian leader of the early twentieth century, R. A. Torrey, decided—at what he understood to be God's direction—to have no salary or regular means of support as a way of coming to know the reality of God's day-to-day provision. He thereafter took no offerings in his meetings and spoke to no human beings about his needs. He lived a public life seen by all, and he reported that day after day, week after week, month after month, year after year, he "walked up to that aperture in Heaven which men call 'prayer'" and asked God for what he needed. It was supplied. The needs of his family and his ministry were more than fully met. He went out of his way to insist that this was not something that every Christian should do, but something he chose to do to verify the present reality of God in his life.[15]

But here again one must say that *no one has to know*. And the fact that there are intelligent people who disagree is simply a part of the world as it has been arranged—perhaps for good reasons. One might well imagine that God allows himself to be known to those who *want* him to be real and want him to be God. That certainly seems to be the biblical picture. But, in any case, disagreement on any matter of great or small significance for human life does *not* mean that knowledge concerning it is impossible or that there is no one who actually has knowledge with respect to it. The standard of knowledge is truth and proper evidence, and there is no necessary correlation between these and agreement, even by "experts."

FOR DISCUSSION

1. "The faith of a Christ follower, defined by the Apostles' Creed, involves particular events and conditions beyond the range of physical nature or natural reality." Is this really true?

2. Are there any "deists" today? Have you ever met one? What might lead someone to be a deist?

3. Would it be beneath God's dignity to intervene in the "course of nature"?

4. What do you think of the idea of a university *committed* to secularism? Is reality secular? Does someone know that it is? Has "research" established it?

5. Under what conditions would a "miracle"—an event outside the course of nature—be impossible?

6. What are the *ultimate* conditions upon which the regularities of nature depend?

7. What do you think of Norwood Hanson's proposal for convincing himself that God exists?

8. How could we know that a particular event was a miracle?

9. How would that method of knowledge apply to the resurrection of Christ?

10. Should professional historians today apply their best tools of research to determine whether Jesus died and rose from the dead? Why should not failure to do so be counted as a failure of professional responsibility on their part?

11. If "experts" fail to know something, does that mean that it is not knowable? That the events or facts in question are not real?

SIX

Knowledge of Christ in the Spiritual Life

But strive first for the kingdom of God and his righteousness, and all these things will be given to you as well.

JESUS, MATTHEW 6:33

THOSE WHO REALLY do know Christ in the modern world
do so by seeking and entering the kingdom of God. Everything else we have discussed here is meant to lead up to that. To
know Christ in the modern world is to know him in *your* world
now. To know him in your world now is *to live interactively with
him right where you are* in your daily activities. This is the *spiritual
life* in Christ. He is, in fact, your contemporary, and he is now
about *his* business of moving humanity along toward its destiny
in this amazing universe. You don't want to miss out on being a
part—*your* part—of that great project. You want to be sure to
take your life into his life, and in that way to find your life to be
"eternal," as God intended it.

There is a real danger that you *will* miss out on this involvement with eternity and thereby miss the entire point of your
existence. Eternity is now in process. Silently it moves along.
But it will not run over you. You have to really want it—deep
down—or you will miss it. That is why Jesus said to seek it more

than anything else. Today, given the prevailing intellectual and cultural atmosphere, you are likely to pick up from your surroundings, with no special thought on your part, the conviction that there is no knowledge to be had of good and evil, no knowledge of God, and no divine presence in our world that enables us to transcend its merciless regularities. If that conviction settles in on you, you will live in terms of it and never enter the kingdom of God. "Let it be done for you according to your faith" (Matt. 8:13).

By now it should be clear that that conviction is not a necessity. You don't have to live in terms of it. There is a difference between good and evil, and it can be known. It is the difference between love, on the one hand, and coldness or indifference culminating in contempt and hatred, on the other. And we can know there is a vast nonphysical ("spiritual") being that overshadows our world, making personal interventions into its grinding regularities quite possible—and sometimes actual. Life does not have to be just what happens "in the course of nature." However, even if all of this is clear, that alone does not constitute knowing *Christ himself*. It only clears the way for such a "knowing" to open up.

MAKING THE KINGDOM OF GOD AVAILABLE

What Jesus did in his special time on earth long ago was to make the kingdom of God, which he also referred to as the "kingdom of the heavens," tangibly present among ordinary human beings. And the people of his time were "ordinary" all right, leading regular human lives. They were just like you and me in that respect. But they had also been prepared as a people, through a long and painful process of historical development, to *tangibly* receive the kingdom of God and to make it accessible to others, even to the whole of humanity. That is what his followers proceeded to do, and their successors are still doing.

When the youngest of Jesus's early friends, John the apostle, had grown old in a life of carrying out the "Jesus project," he reflected in amazement on what had come to pass with him and the others:

What started it all, what we heard and we saw with our own eyes, what we observed and our hands handled concerning The Word of Life—for *the* life was put right out in the open before us, and we saw it, and now we testify to its reality and announce to you the eternal life which was at home in God the Father and was set right before our eyes—what we saw and heard, we also pass on to you that you too may be in this together with us, and we really are in it with the Father and with his Son, Jesus the Anointed One. And our writing to you about these things tops off the joy we have in them. (1 John 1:1–4, paraphrase)

KNOWLEDGE BY "ACQUAINTANCE"

Knowledge "at a distance," knowing certain "facts" about something, doesn't amount to knowing *it*. It therefore does not have the same power over life. In philosophy we rightly distinguish knowledge by *description* from knowledge by *acquaintance*. Only the latter is the interactive relationship, the "reality hook," that gives us a grasp of the person or the thing "itself." Out of his own experience Job characteristically remarked to God: "I have heard about you . . . but now my eye sees you. So I take back all I said, and I repent by throwing dust and ashes upon myself" (Job 42:5–6, paraphrase).

Thomas, another of the early friends of Jesus, heard *about* his being alive after his crucifixion, but that was not enough for him. He wanted to *touch* the wounds. Touch is one main way we supplement sight and fill in the reality of something seen. He is often called "doubting Thomas," with some scorn. But it was Jesus's idea to include the senses in the disciples' knowledge of his postcrucifixion body. When he earlier met the other disciples after his death, "he showed them his hands and his side," and "the disciples rejoiced when they *saw* the Lord" (John 20:20). Jesus welcomed Thomas's touch upon his wounds, though it appears that Thomas didn't really require that after all, once he had seen the Lord (vv. 28–29). Certainly John the apostle had such scenes as these in mind when he speaks as he does above of "handling" the Word of Life with his hands.

SPIRITUAL LIFE: FIRSTHAND INTERACTION

The way of Jesus Christ is a way of *firsthand interaction*—knowing by acquaintance—direct awareness of him and his kingdom. Rarely will it involve anything like the sense perception of the Eternal provided to John and Thomas and the other apostles of Jesus. But you can't really sustain a kingdom life, a life "not of this world," without such interaction with the King. And such an interaction with God is the most precious thing available to any human being. It simply *is* eternal life (John 17:3). Thus Paul, the "come lately" apostle, says, "I regard everything as loss because of the surpassing value of knowing Christ Jesus my Lord!" His highest objective in life—even when long past the point where one might think he had "arrived"—was "to know Christ and the power of his resurrection and the sharing of his sufferings by becoming like him in his death, if somehow I may attain the resurrection from the dead" (Phil. 3:8–11).

What Paul is talking about is exactly what Jesus had in mind when he said, "Strive first for the kingdom of God and his righteousness, and all these things will be given to you as well" (Matt. 6:33). The great difference is that by the time it gets to Paul and to an older John, they understand much more precisely what Jesus meant by these words from his Sermon on the Mount and how to do what he said. Jesus is the human face on the kingdom of God. He makes it concretely accessible.

Now, in the historical rise of the situation we are dealing with in this book, *the displacement of Christian knowledge into the domain of mere belief and tradition,* the difference between a religion of mere facts, however holy the facts, and a dynamic religion of interactive fellowship in which Christ alive played a huge role. Serious and thoughtful people as well as the careless were turned away from the kingdom of God "at hand," because what was presented to them, intentionally or not, as his way of life was understood to be mere belief in facts *about* him—almost totally facts of long ago. And often the choice they were confronted with was whether they would believe the historical miracles rightly associated with the Christian faith. If they said they could not believe, they were then commonly told they could not be Christians. That is why the issue of the reality of miracles and of the obligation to believe in them (see the Apostles' Creed), became *the* issues for faith and nonfaith in the nineteenth century, and why it remains so today, both in "respectable" intellectual circles and in conflicts about who is and who is not "orthodox."

Gotthold Lessing, a famous literary figure of the eighteenth century, complained that mere belief in the historical miracles did not bring to life the central truths of Christianity for today. He thought that "the truth of these [historical] miracles has completely ceased to be demonstrable by miracles still happening now."[1] He famously remarked on "the ugly, broad ditch, which I cannot get across," between truths about past miracles, on the one hand, and living now in a world where God is active in my life, on the other—living, that is, the life we *ought* to live according to the very ethical teachings of Jesus himself. Those teachings have come down to us in many traditional ways and remain present to us in the contemporary world. It is this contemporary world where we must meet him and know him if we are to meet and know him at all. But we certainly can live out those teachings in real life *only if we are living in the kingdom of God with him.* This must be our experiential reality. On that point, Lessing was surely correct.

THE POWER OF OUR SOCIAL VISION

But the breakthrough to Jesus himself now faces many obstacles. The well-known sociologist Peter Berger presents a fascinating discussion of how we all live encapsulated in a vision of who we are and what is "real" in our social setting. This vision, however, is a "precarious perspective," as he calls it, which may abandon us or slip over into another "vision" strongly opposed to the one we previously lived in. Obviously this can be a devastating "alteration." It may be precipitated by terrible events, such as a war, profound moral confusions or failures, or painful personal calamities. Such an "alteration" can also be liberating, but it is always upsetting. Berger provides many illustrations.

There have in fact been earthshaking "alterations" in Western society over the last two centuries. In the light of them, Berger considers the question: *Can a truly contemporary person be a Christian?* Many Europeans, he notes, will answer, "Of course *not*!"[2] They have had a culture-wide "alteration" from past ages and have "seen through" the vision of traditional Christian reality. The brutal events of the twentieth century have brought that about. The "world taken for granted" by generations past, and still by many contemporary Christians in America today, can no longer be taken seriously by decent, intelligent people. The Apostles' Creed is on a level with the flat earth. So it is often assumed now.

It is assumed, at least in part, because religion in general and the Christian version in particular have been complicit in so much of the evil prevalent in past and present societies. "It is not by chance," Berger says, "that religious people are more likely to believe in society as it is taken for granted than those who have emancipated themselves from religion. . . . Religion appears over and over again as that which validates the carnival of masks" worn by those who play out the roles dictated by social "reality."[3] Religion upholds a vision of "how things are" in a society that is shot through with evil, and thus religion becomes subject to ethical condemnation. It appears to those not totally caught up in it as an *indecency*. Thus "decent" persons cannot be Christians. It is repeatedly pointed out that religious wars, the Crusades, slavery, and repression have been sanctioned and sustained by Christians. And "God" has allowed the terrible secular wars and disasters of recent decades. How can a "decent" person accept that?

JESUS HIMSELF

At this point Berger takes a surprising turn. Instead of simply adopting the atheist rejection of religion, so common among sociologists and others who think of themselves as intellectuals, he points

> to the only Christian resolution of our argument that we can find—a confrontation of our perception of society with the figure of Jesus Christ. It is this figure of the crucified one which continues to haunt both the oppressors and the oppressed, casting its shadow over the religious celebrations and at the same time intruding its disturbing light into the corners where one escapes the sacred drums. . . . We now find that it is not enough to perceive society and religion, but we are compelled to relate this perception to a demand that transcends both society and religion—the demand to follow this figure of the crucified one. This demand calls us to an exodus, not only out of the Egypt of social mythology but also out of the Zion of religious security. The exodus takes us out of the holy city, out past the scene of cross and resurrection, and beyond into the desert in which God is waiting. In this desert all horizons are open.[4]

We, somehow, move beyond precarious social or cultural "visions" as we live in the presence of Jesus.

I have to say that this is one of the most surprising turns I have ever found in sociological or other academic writing. But Berger is right. *Jesus comes through* in spite of everything. The most profound critic of society and the "masks," Christian and otherwise, is Jesus himself. In this respect he stands in the line of the sharp-tongued Hebrew prophets and brings it to completion. Berger finds that "the crucial point of the relationship between Christian faith and the antireligious critique is to be found in a theological proposition. The proposition states that the revelation of God in Jesus Christ (which is the object of Christian faith) is something very different from religion."[5] Religion has many critics, but Jesus very few. He is a self-authenticating reality beyond the myriad social cocoons. He belongs to humanity. He called himself "Son of Man."

Berger thus aligns his view of Jesus with the names of Dietrich Bonhoeffer, Simone Weil, and Søren Kierkegaard as well as Karl Barth. These people have testified to a Christ that transcends all social visions and all entanglements with religion. In him God breaks through. "Christian faith is not religion," Berger affirms.[6] That is the scalding truth of the matter. Suddenly from under the smothering panoply of human visions there emerges an outbreak of realism—a little breath of something that promises to interrupt and stand in judgment upon all our enculturated "visions" and their possible "alterations" of one into another. It is the Jesus of "all nations," of "all ethnic groups," of all kinds of people, of "whosoever will"—of the last who are first and the first who are last in human orders. He is the light that gives light to everyone who is in the world.

HE SUCCEEDS IN BEING PRESENT IN OUR WORLD

How are we to think about Jesus's presence today? No doubt volumes could be written on that question, and have been. But the simple fact is that *Jesus Christ is present in this world*, the only world we have, and in many ways. His teachings, even mangled and broken, have an incredible power to disrupt human systems, including the ones that claim to own him. He is *the* misfit and thus is available to all who would seek him. His crucifixion and resurrection announce the end of human systems and stand in judgment over them. He is the man on the cross calling us to join him there. He makes himself available to individuals who hear of him and seek him. In many forms both inside and outside the church, with its traditions, symbolisms, and literature, he is simply here among us. He is in his people, but he does not allow himself to be boxed in by them. He calls to us by just being here in our midst. There is nothing like him. The people in the churches also have the option of finding him and following him into his kingdom, though that may rarely be what they are doing.

For many today who think of themselves as educated, historical studies and "higher criticism"—perhaps something they call a "scientific" outlook—have made the person and teachings of Jesus problematic. From where they start, he seems a questionable resource for actually living their lives. He may become for them a scholarly football to kick around or to ignore. But he does not go away. In spite of all, he himself is still available in this world, and beyond all historical issues and confusions there stands a strong if somewhat hazy impression of what he stood for. To come to know him and to clarify who he really is, people have only *to stand for what he stood for,* as best they can, and to do so by *inviting him to take their life into his life and walk with them.* If they do just this with humility and openness—which everyone knows to be his manner of life—they will know him more and more as they take his life to be their life. In this way they do not have to "know" at the start. It is enough to *venture* on the kingdom of God and its King. "Everyone who calls on the name of the Lord shall be saved" (Acts 2:21).

PAST ALL BARRIERS

The German theologian Wilhelm Herrmann remarked:

> Jesus intended to do more than make the best ideal clear for men, and more than live it out before them. As the Messiah, He claimed not merely to set men a task, but to give to them God's perfect gift. He was confident that He could so influence men that they would be enabled for a life of power. The Jesus who thinks thus of Himself, and who looks on humanity with such a confidence in His power to redeem them from the terrible misery in which He sees everyone round about Him, stands as a fact before us, a fact that has no equal.[7]

Hermann was especially concerned to stress that the scholarly results of "higher criticism" of the Bible and any results of genuine science do not shut the Christ of the Bible off from humanity. Jesus himself comes through and affirms his reality in the "communion of the Christian with God."

It is possible for religious people, and Christians in particular, to follow Jesus into the kingdom of God and come to know Christ in the modern world. All that is necessary is that they come to realize that they have not "arrived" by means of their particular identification as "Christians" or otherwise, and that they be willing to make *knowing the kingdom* their first priority. Then their confidence in Jesus—if it really is confidence in *him*, not just in something he did or said—can lead them into increasing knowledge of him. Their pride in orthodoxy (left or right) or in the form of religion they are practicing is their greatest danger, but it too can be overcome by paying attention to Jesus himself. Speaking from the very center of the bewilderments of contemporary thought, A. N. Wilson remarked that he cannot ". . . think that our own age has a monopoly of wisdom, and it will take more than a handful of textual critics or analytic philosophers to demolish the experience of those millions of men and women who, in all corners of the earth, and for nearly two thousand years, have been able to echo the excited words of the Apostle Andrew: 'We have discovered the Messias (which means the Christ).' "[8]

A REMARKABLE CASE

Frank Laubach was one of the great Christ followers of the twentieth century. He finished his education at Union Theological Seminary and Columbia University and then taught for a number of years in a Christian seminary in the Philippines. Disappointed in his hopes for leadership at the seminary, he went to live among the Maranao people on the island of Lanao. There he sought God as never before, and he found him. He was guided into a practice of constant fellowshiping with God through listening for him, speaking to him about whatever was being done at the moment and what was in his heart, and finding God acting *with* him as he went through his daily activities. With much effort and practice he trained himself to bring God, and what is of God, back before his mind every minute or so, and from this he constantly drank in power to guide and strengthen himself. His account of how this grew and became his usual way of living is contained in letters to his father between January 3, 1930, and January 2, 1932, published under the title *Letters by a Modern Mystic*.[9] God gave him, among other things, a technique of teaching others to read, starting from their spoken language. He founded the World Literacy Crusade and became a statesman for Christ around the world. Laubach says:

> As for me, I never lived, I was half dead, I was a rotting tree, until I reached the place where I wholly, with utter honesty, resolved and then re-resolved that I *would* find

God's will, and I *would* do that will though every fiber in me said no, and I *would* win the battle in my thoughts. It was as though some deep artesian well had been struck in my soul . . . and strength came forth. I do not claim success even for a day yet—in my mind, not complete success all day—but some days are close to success, and every day is tingling with the joy of a glorious discovery. That thing is eternal. That thing is undefeatable. . . . This spirit which comes to a mind set upon continuous surrender, this spirit is timeless life.[10]

How practical is this for the average human being? Laubach asked. He answers:

It seems to me now that yonder plowman could be like Calixto Sanidad, when he was a lonesome and mistreated plowboy, "with my eyes on the furrow, and my hands on the lines, but my thoughts on God." The carpenter could be as full of God as was Christ when he drove nails. The millions at looms and lathes could make the hours glorious. Some hour spent by some night watchman might be the most glorious ever lived on earth.[11]

PRACTICAL STEPS TO KINGDOM LIVING

But how are we to enter into this interactive relationship of knowing Christ that is life with him in the kingdom of God? There are two preliminaries that must be observed if we are to enter the interactive life with Jesus Christ and, through him, with God.

Humility: The first one is, very simply, we must humble ourselves and become like little children (Matt. 18:3–5). That means we must be turned around ("converted") from the normal human attitude, the attitude that says *we* are in charge of our life and that we are quite competent and capable of managing it on our own. Little children, on the other hand, come to others for guidance and help and simply presume upon them for it. They have no other option, and they do not think they do—in spite of occasional outbursts of what in adults might be called "self-will."

Now, for many people, perhaps for most, that will simply be the end of the story. They are not going to humble themselves. That would be beneath their dignity. Or they may try to "negotiate a deal with God" in which they are still the ones in charge of their lives and just occasionally get at little help from him for some of *their* projects. It simply doesn't work that way, however. They will never come to *know* the reality of the kingdom or the King if that remains their approach. Any efforts they make in such an approach will meet with a blank wall.

Jesus told a story about two men who went "to church" to pray (Luke 18:9–14). One thought very well of himself and "thanked *God*" (can you believe it?) that he was not like other people—especially not like that crook the tax man, standing over there by himself. For his part, the tax man stood with downcast eyes, unwilling even to look up at heaven. He was deeply ashamed of himself. In agony he perhaps jerked out some of his own hair and repeatedly slapped himself ("beat his breast"), saying, "God, be merciful to me, a disgusting wretch!" Jesus pointed out that the tax man went home accepted by God, while the other man did not. "All who exalt themselves will be humbled," he said, "but all who humble themselves will be exalted." We need to reflect deeply on what this says about the nature of God.

What is this about? Only the humble person will let God be God. Such people are *realistic* about who they actually are (none of Peter Berger's "masks"). A proper sense of human sinfulness and inadequacy *may* bring people to humility, though for those still set against God, it will not do so. It will only make them more hostile and defiant toward God, and perhaps greater hypocrites, hiding who they really are. We don't get God's attention by doing him favors and "looking good." He doesn't need that. Through Isaiah God says, "But this is the one to whom I will look, to the humble and contrite in spirit, who trembles at my word" (66:2). "Trust in the Lord with all your heart," Proverbs says, "and do not rely on your own insight. In all your ways acknowledge him, and he will make straight your paths. Do not be wise in your own eyes; fear the Lord and turn away from evil" (3:5–6). Turning away from evil is itself an act of humility, for to choose evil is *always* a matter of doing what *I* want in dependence on me.

Inward rightness: The second preliminary to entering the interactive life with Christ is closely related to the first. It is the decision and the settled intention, carried into practice, to become good, "righteous," *on the inside*—in the hidden dimensions of the self that make up human character—not just in action or outward behavior. This is what Jesus called going beyond the "goodness" characteristic of the "scribes (scholars) and the Pharisees." He said that "unless your goodness surpasses that of the scribes and Pharisees, you shall not enter the kingdom of the heavens" (Matt. 5:20, paraphrase). "Entering the kingdom of the heavens," as here spoken of, is clearly not a matter of "making it into heaven" after death—though it takes care of that at the appropriate time. It is precisely a matter of *being interactively engaged with the kingdom in your life now.*

That interaction is God's gift of himself to human beings elsewhere referred to as "the birth from above" (John 3:3, 5). You cannot earn this, but you do have to actively receive it. You do that by welcoming God into every dimension of your character and life, holding nothing back. It is to be total surrender. God is actually looking for people who will do this. He is seeking those who will worship him "in spirit and truth" (John 4:23–24). It will take some time to overcome the habits of deceit and manipulation that are rooted in the inward person, heart, mind, body. But to know Christ in the kingdom of God we must abandon ourselves to a total transformation of *who we are on the inside,* to taking on the character of Christ through living with him day by day and hour by hour. Only that is trust in Christ.

OBEDIENCE WHERE WE ARE

With these two preliminaries in place—and when they are in place we will certainly be aware that God is acting in us—we grow in our knowledge of Christ-with-us by, first of all, constant expectation of him *in the place where we are,* wherever that may be. "The sacrament of the present moment," as it is sometimes called, is from the human side nothing but the *invocation, expectation, and receptivity of God's presence and activity where we are and in what we are doing at any given time.* Then we steadily grow in graceful interactions with Father, Son, and Holy Spirit. They gradually take up all of our life into their trinitarian life (John 17:21–24).

Among the many misunderstandings Jesus had to counteract in his teaching was the one that held the kingdom to be some gigantic event in some special place. This was human thinking about *human* kingdoms, which always fit that description. He was constantly faced with people who wanted to know when the kingdom of God was coming. When is the big commotion? He patiently replied that the kingdom of God was not that kind of thing. It was simply God reigning, governing. It is not a special event you could see happening over here or possibly over there. "Now look," he said, "the kingdom of God is right here among you" (Luke 17:20–21, paraphrase). His main sermon line was: "Get a new thought! The kingdom of the heavens is available to you from right where you are!" (Matt. 4:17, paraphrase).

This actually was not a new biblical teaching. The ancient book of Deuteronomy had said:

The Lord will again take delight in prospering you, just as he delighted in prospering your ancestors, when . . . you turn to the Lord your God with all your heart and with all your soul. Surely, this commandment I am commanding you today is not too hard for you, nor is it too far away. It is not in heaven, that you should say, "Who will go up to heaven for us, and get it for us so that we may hear it and observe it?" Neither is it beyond the sea, that you should say, "Who will cross to the other side of the sea for us, and get it for us so we may hear it and observe it?" No, the word is very near to you; it is in your mouth and in your heart for you to observe. (30:9–14)

This fundamental truth about *life in God* is given its full meaning by Paul: "If you confess with your lips that Jesus as Lord and believe in your heart that God raised him from the dead, you will be saved" (Rom. 10:9). But that is not a thing you *say* to get you into heaven after death. It is what you do to live in Christ's *kingdom now*. What is saved is our life, and of course we along with it.

Now, once you have received God into the place where you are at any and all times, you are ready, next, to *do what pleases God* on every occasion. Without him with you, you could never do that. The "with God" grounds the "do God." From where we are coming as human beings, obeying Christ is really pretty scary and may cost us dearly, even to the point of losing our lives. But with him with us, we become able to see and do what is best. From the human side, once again, it is a matter of deciding to do the things Jesus said—really a matter of deciding, by God's grace, to become the kind of person who does what he said. That immediately draws us into the context of *his* action where we know the eternal life flowing in us and around us. This is the spiritual life in Christ.

IT'S ALL ABOUT *AGAPE* LOVE

So Jesus told us: "If you love me, you will keep my commandments. And I will ask the Father, and he will give you another Strengthener [the Holy Spirit], to be with you forever" (John

14:15–16, paraphrase). And again: "They who have my commandments and keep them are those who love me; and those who love me shall be loved by my Father, and I will love them and reveal myself to them. . . . My Father will love them, and we will come to them and make our home with them" (14:21, 23). The interactive relationship in which we know Christ beyond all "masks" is the very atmosphere in which those who keep his commands live constantly.

We know that the nature of this life is love. As friends of Christ we love God with all our heart, soul, mind, and strength, and our neighbor as ourself (Mark 12:29–31). At least that is what our heart is set on learning, and we are making steady progress. Old John says: "Beloved, let us love one another, because love is from God; everyone who loves is born of God and knows God" (1 John 4:7). Of course, "love" here is not the thing that lives in human fantasy and whimsy, song and saga. Love promotes the good of what is loved. Love is defined by the person and the teachings of Christ. Love is the source of the distinction between good and evil, right and wrong, as we discussed in Chapter 3.

Love means that we humbly and simply devote ourselves under God to the promotion of the goods of human life that come under our influence. We live to serve. We do this expecting God to intervene with us to produce an outcome that is beyond all human ability, and we do it knowing that God is the one "watching our back." We cast all our "care" on him, knowing he is the one who takes care of us (Ps. 55:22; 1 Pet. 5:5–7). In that way we *know* God—and do remember, *knowing* is our topic—through doing the good called for by love. We will experience a power of a life not of ourselves. That is, precisely, God in action that we are experiencing.

THE PLACE OF "SPIRITUAL DISCIPLINES"
IN KNOWING CHRIST

I have given two preliminaries and two substantial elements of living life with Jesus in the kingdom of God. These are, respectively, *humility* and the *intention of inward transformation,* and the *practice of Christ's constant presence* and progressive overall *obedience.* Let us call these, taken together, the "Christ focus." For the sake of clarity it is important to put the matter in this straightforward way. We must make no mistake about what goes into a life of knowing Christ in the modern world.

But it is also important to understand that *in practice* we will have to *learn* to lead an ordered life centered on those four things: humility, pursuit of inward transformation, constant receptivity to the "Presence," and unqualified obedience to Jesus. There is some latitude for cultural variations and individual peculiarities in the learning process, but that process is unavoidable and must be embraced. We have to *learn* to do the things that eliminate distractions and keep our whole being focused upon constant companionship with Christ in our "nows." In this way the life of a *disciple* of Jesus—of his *student* or *apprentice* in kingdom living—takes its individualized shape. And to come to him in faith *is* to enroll as his disciple. It is constantly to go to school under his tutelage. Anything less than that simply misses him and reveals we do not actually have faith in him. But as disciples our faith grows as our knowledge grows. There are some time-tested spiritual practices that can help us in our learning process.

Solitude and silence. Among the practices that we learn to engage in to enable effectual focus upon Christ is a combination of solitude and silence. You have only to look at the lives of those most successful in living with Christ to see that this is so. To go into solitude means to be alone and do nothing for lengthy periods of time. That is necessary to break the grip of a God-alienated world over us at the level of our constant habits and preoccupations. Silence means to eliminate noise, including the noise of our own mouth. It further frees us to move into the life that is eternal. We need to combine solitude and silence on some occasions to gain their full effects. They must be practiced intensely and extensively.

These are root-reaching practices that slowly bring us to an understanding of who and what we really are—often producing occasions of profound repentance—and that allow God to reoccupy the places in our lives where only he belongs. They require lengthy times and extreme intensity to do their work, though at the beginning we must ease into them in a gentle and nonheroic manner. Once established in our mind, soul, body, and social involvements, they go with us wherever we are and need to be renewed only periodically by special times of practice. Irritability and anger, loneliness and busyness, are signs that they need renewal.

Fellowship with other disciples, living and dead, is another practice essential to the "Christ focus." Some with whom we must have fellowship have been long dead, but they live on and are available to us through writings. Of course, many of these are in the Bible. Others are nearer to us in time, and some are our contemporaries. We need to devote much time to knowing them well. We must above all master the masters.[12] Spiritual reading is one of the major sources of light and strength for the disciple of Jesus. But, as valuable as it is, it cannot take the place of fellowship with other disciples living and walking beside us.

When we gather "in the name" of Jesus, we gather to love one another and to be loved, to serve one another and be served. That is why we "go to church." The one sure mark of being his disciple was said by Jesus to be that we love one another in the way he loves us (John 13:34–35). He was prepared to say that you cannot receive *his kind of love* in your approach to people from anyone else. No one else can bring us there. That is the only Christian exclusiveness, and it is an exclusiveness that takes care of itself. We do not have to "enforce" it. So when we "go to church," we go to love those who are there and to be loved with his *agape* love. But that love is not confined to when we are "in church." It is for everywhere in life. Church is for catching it and practicing it.

It is of absolute importance that you get this right if you are to *know* Christ. We know Christ in others. Reflect on what goes on within you upon first sighting another disciple. It may be a member of your family or someone at your job, or it may be as you approach your meeting place (your "church"). Is your first thought that they should be blessed by God in every way? That they should be "better" than you are ("In humility regard others as better than yourselves" Phil. 2:3)? Are you prepared to serve them spiritually by lifting them to God in prayer for his utmost gifts to them and by assisting them in their needs? Do you earnestly long that *their* light should shine in such a way that others would see their good works and glorify God because of them? (Matt. 5:16). It is out of such a heart and overall disposition that we spontaneously and without thinking "rejoice with those who rejoice, weep with those who weep" (Rom. 12:15). Or do we meet others more in the spirit of the Pharisee who prayed alongside the tax man?

The most important thing about our fellowship with other disciples is that Jesus, the trinitarian presence, should be in our midst. For that, we must meet "in his name" (Matt. 18:19); that is, we meet for his purposes, with his resources, and in his presence. This will no doubt require some serious readjustments, given how "church" is generally practiced today. But it can be done if you and I are willing to walk with Jesus in doing it and not get caught up in superiority and in condemnatory comparisons as we look upon those around us—and especially upon those who do not agree with us or even attack us.

If we come together in this way, Jesus's idea of evangelism and "mission" will fall into place: "I in them and you in me, that they may become completely one, so that the world may *know* [there's that word again] that you have sent me and have loved them even as you have loved me" (John 17:23). As Frank Laubach says: "The simple program of Christ for winning the whole world is to make each person he touches magnetic enough with love to draw others."[13] If we grow our fellowship in this direction, it will naturally affect those around us, whether in the fellowship or not. This kind of love and the "Presence" go with us wherever we go. They cannot be hidden. A "missional church," in a wording often used today, is actually one that cannot be stopped from increasing, because it grows by contiguity—skin on skin.

A RANGE OF SPIRITUAL DISCIPLINES

Solitude, silence, and fellowship are among what we call "spiritual disciplines." This is not the place for a full treatment of the disciplines for the spiritual life "in Christ,"[14] but the fundamental idea of *growing in the "Christ focus"* through *specific practices* is absolutely *crucial* to knowing Christ in the contemporary world. Spiritual disciplines are things we can do to increase our receptivity to grace. Grace is God acting in our lives to accomplish what we cannot do on our own. The "Christ focus" is sustained and developed by shaping our lives, with his help, around definite and time-proven practices that enable us to be kingdom people: to live in the "Presence" and to obey his teachings from the inside out. Not only solitude and silence and fellowship, of the type described, but also service, study, worship, prayer, confession, fasting, frugality, and submission, among other things, have proven to be ways of turning our entire being toward God, and through him back to the world in the goodness of a God-filled life. These practices are not ways of earning favor from or impressing either God or other people. They are simply wise ways of opening ourselves to the "Presence" ever more fully. They are avenues of knowing Christ now.

Prayer and giving are of special importance for knowing Christ in life with him, a "knowing" that reaches far beyond their highly effective disciplinary benefits. *Prayer* is God's arrangement for a safe *power sharing* with us in his intention to bless the world through us. In response to prayer we see good accomplished far beyond what we are capable of and in a form suited to the wisdom of God—not just to what we think *we* know about the situation we are praying for. Clearly prayer is a major dimension of living interactively with God.

Giving is, among other things, an exercise in turning loose of what we have in our little "kingdom" to enter into the amazing reciprocity that God has built into the human heart.[15] "Give," Jesus said, "and it will be given to you. A good measure, pressed down, shaken together, running over, will be put into your lap; for the measure you give will be the measure you get back" (Luke 6:38). Note that it "will be given" to you—others around you will give to you. Generosity is what people are made for. They would love to be generous—if only they thought they *could*. Of course, they will rarely know they actually can unless they are *experiencing* life in the kingdom of God. Generosity is one essential dimension of love, and there is ample provision for it. Start being generous with what you have and it will grow. Prayer and giving are the first two concrete ways of venturing on the kingdom of God and finding its reality.

NO FORMULA, ONLY A LIFE

In spite of the recommendations above, there is no formulaic or mechanical way of specifying the things we do to enter the interactive life in the kingdom of God. I have only given some suggestions that have proven useful. Kingdom life is, after all, a *personal* relationship of "knowing by acquaintance," and as such it is developed in personal encounters and in "back and forth" exchanges over a temporal process of some length. One *grows* "in the grace and knowledge of our Lord and Savior Jesus Christ" (2 Pet. 3:18). Knowledge is interactive relationship, and grace is God acting in our lives.

There is nothing intrinsically mysterious about the "with God" life. It looks mysterious only to those who do not want it or who, for whatever reasons, will not take the simple steps toward it. Frank Laubach, once again, really wanted it, as have multitudes of others, and they have found it. Of such people the word is spoken: "Ask, and it will be given to you; seek, and you will find; knock, and the door will be opened to you. For everyone who asks receives, and everyone who searches finds, and for everyone who knocks the door will be opened" (Matt. 7:7–8). If, after some serious effort, you find that this is "not working" for you, stand back and reflect on what part of what you are seeking is not really wanted or what part of you does not want God's way. That is proven to be a necessary element of the growth process for those who really want to know Christ as living reality. No one can avoid it. It is a voyage in profound self-discovery.

WHAT'S IT REALLY LIKE?

What will you experience as you come to know Christ in your world? We must not leave our present topic without being very clear on this matter. It concerns the *verifiability* of claims made about the spiritual life in Christ. Those "living the life" will:

1. *Discover remarkable changes in their beliefs, fundamental attitudes, and emotional conditions.* Remember, from our earlier discussions, what belief is. It is a readiness to act as if what is believed were so. Living the life, people find that they are ready to act as if Jesus Christ actually is Lord, Master of the universe. This is a fact about themselves they will find astonishing, and one they will "confess" or "own up to." Associated with that

new and emerging belief will be a remarkable change in their emotional condition. Most prominent in the new condition will be hopefulness, naturally accompanied by joy and peace. One of Paul's prayers expresses this new condition: "May the God of hope fill you with all joy and peace in believing, so that you may abound in hope by the power of the Holy Spirit" (Rom. 15:13). And again he says, "The kingdom of God is not food and drink but righteousness and peace and joy in the Holy Spirit" (Rom. 14:17).

2. *Receive "communications" from God.* By far most of these communications will come in conjunction with study of the Bible, and they will always be consistent with what is taught in the Bible. But in living the life people will need directions about things of which the Bible says nothing: the particular circumstances, events, and choices they are facing and particular insights into truths. They will learn to identify a characteristic kind of thought or experience that comes to them from God. They will find themselves "spoken to" and taught about many things, and these "communications" will be testable against the realities of life and the insights of others. This is a matter that must be dealt with carefully, and in utmost humility and openness. But it is a real and indispensable part of "the life."[16]

3. *Discover the reality of "the light burden and the easy yoke"* (Matt. 11:28–30). That is, people will find that "Someone" is *acting with them.* They will find that what they have to do does not crush them, and that the outcomes of their efforts far exceed anything that could be humanly anticipated. This will be the regular quality of their life and not just a rare, hit-or-miss condition that cannot be counted on.

These three features of spiritual life in Christ are imprecise—cannot be put into strictly quantitative terms—but they are real and can be verified. They are, as wise Aristotle used to say, "true on the whole and for the most part." As such they can be verified to the satisfaction of any fair-minded persons willing to consider the facts of the case. "Real effects have real causes," as William James points out.[17] The quality of life in Christ is available for all who will to know, and it clearly falls in the domain of the miraculous.

CRITICS OF GOD AND KNOWLEDGE OF GOD

In recent years we have seen a number of atheistic writers contesting the existence of God and the knowledge of God. Much can be learned from them, and we should learn what we can. But it seems fairly obvious that they are simply ignorant of what we have been talking about in this chapter: the spiritual life in Christ. They literally do not know what they are talking about when it comes to knowing Christ as a life that some people actually live. They have not taken the trouble to understand even what they could know as "outsiders" by sympathetically studying the lives of the great "insiders." It is very likely that they consider it all bunk because, they think, they know there is no God, and hence no knowledge of God and no "interactive life" with him. So what the great (and small) insiders know of the spiritual life in Christ must be only a delusion.

But it is clear that these critics do not long for there to be a biblical type of God or to be a part of his life. It is not something they would welcome. They do not seriously study the spiritual life in those who actually live it. They content themselves with psychological "explanations" of the "saints" they happen to know about, with citations of what "science says," and with making various points against arguments for the existence and knowledge of God. Now, whatever truly valid points they have to make will stand. We want nothing else. As Christ followers we want every-thing be exactly what it is. But it remains that these critics really do not know what they are talking about, and do not want to know when it comes to spiritual life in Christ. "Let it be done for them according to their faith." God is not going to prove himself by running over them. That is not his way. And if he did run over them, they would not know what hit them.

The proposal by Norwood Hanson, which we looked at in the last chapter, is painfully typical of the crude images of God and the worship of God against which our popular atheists define themselves. Those images make nonsense of any spiritual life for believers. The appalling but self-confident "theologies" of atheists and agnostics do much to explain what they get so excited about. I, for one, would hope that Hanson would *not* believe that what he (in imagination) saw—the "Zeus-like" figure—was God. If he were to believe in *that* "god," he would simply be another idolater. Just imagine what his *devotion* to his "god" could amount to. And of course he would not believe at all if what he described were all there was to the show. He would perhaps be befuddled for a while, and then he would either take a pill, head for the psychiatrist, or try to get that "god" to do another stunt. His contempt for the very idea of God is shown by the silliness of the scene he sets up.

Our popular atheists today are, generally speaking, uneducated or miseducated people with higher degrees and, in some cases, with striking accomplishments in some specialization. They seem to believe that their attainments license them to talk grandly about things about which they have not informed themselves. However well intended, they stay at the level of superficial intel-lectual debates about the existence of God and knowledge of God and have never made a serious study of theology, Jesus himself, or the Christian spiritual life. At least they give no evidence of it.

A few have delved into "meditation," some other "spiritual" activity, or "religion and the brain" and consequently assume that they understand "spirituality." But the "god" they usually have in mind is certainly not worthy of sympathetic study. And that they could become the kind of person who would live the spiritual life in Christ—Teresa of Avila, Francis de Sales, George Müller, Dorothy Day, Dietrich Bonhoeffer, or Frank Laubach, for example—is surely beyond their comprehension, and certainly beyond their desires. That they do not know Christ in the modern world or think it worth their while to do so is understandable. But it is also of no significance for those who *would* really like to know him. There is no serious reason to think that they have any significant standing in the subject matter upon which they are declaiming or that they should be taken seriously. They are just preaching to their particular choir—a practice deplorably common in the intellectual and academic world as well as in religion.

Their case is rhetorically strengthened in the public arena by the fact that those who self-identify in our culture as Christians often *know* no more about the interactive life with Christ in the kingdom of God than the atheists do and do not manifest that life to the public. They are in many cases only "nominal" Christians who in reality have little or nothing to do with the kingdom of God. They are in no position to respond to the atheists. To "reply" to the atheists and agnostics we need to take them in all intellectual seriousness, hold them rationally responsible for what they say, and lovingly deal with them in the currency of honest intellectual work. As followers of Christ we claim them as friends in the pursuit of knowledge. That should go without saying, but unfortunately it does not. We must do more, however. We must show the reality they deny.

The deeper issue here is the *authority* of the "knowledge institutions" of our time and what shall and shall not be taught under the flag of that authority. Our atheist and agnostic critics *lay claim to that authority,* and their claim must not go uncontested. It is a clearly invalid claim. But beyond that, we must embody the character (intelligent love) and power of life in union with Christ in all aspects of human existence. That is how other people are to be brought to know life in the kingdom if they are to know it at all. If only the intellectual issues are met, that alone will leave people stranded in a life away from God. To know Christ in the contemporary world our opponents must see people and communities of people in which he lives today.

FOR DISCUSSION

1. Describe some cases in which you knew *about* something, but didn't really *know* it. Do the same for some cases in your religious life.

2. Have you had any experience with people who think being a Christian is something degrading or even immoral, who despise Christians as "indecent"?

3. Do you agree with Berger and Hermann that Jesus still manages to "get though" to people in our Western culture in spite of all the historical and scholarly barriers?

4. Could Laubach's experience and testimony apply to you and your life?

5. What is your practical understanding of humility, becoming like "little children," and entering the kingdom of the heavens (Matt. 18:3–4)? Do you know of anyone who has actually become like a little child and entered the kingdom? Have you?

6. In what ways could one go beyond the goodness of scribes and Pharisees (Matt. 5:20)?

7. What would it be like to practice the presence of Christ in real life? Could you give some concrete illustrations or tell a story of it actually happening?

8. Have you experienced the power of some spiritual discipline? How did it work?

9. What is "going to church" like for you? How would you like it to be different?

10. Did you find the three points under "What's It Really Like?" adequate to characterize life with God in the kingdom?

SEVEN

Knowledge of Christ and Christian Pluralism

> I truly understand that God shows no partiality, but in
> every nation anyone who fears him and does what is right
> is acceptable to him.
>
> PETER, ACTS 10:34–35

C HRISTIAN PLURALISM" HERE means a pluralism derived from the understanding of God brought to earth by
Jesus Christ, that is, *a pluralism based upon the generosity and justice
of the God revealed in Christ.* Such a pluralism seems impossible
to many. If Christians and Christian teachers have *knowledge* of
essential points about God, Jesus Christ, and his spiritual life,
that can only mean that those who disagree with them on those
points must be mistaken. That seems unavoidable, a mere matter
of logic. But by an unwarranted transition that has become cus-
tomary today, this is taken to mean that Christians think they
are *better* human beings than those who disagree with them and,
conversely, that those who disagree with them are *inferior,* not as
good, not equal.[1]

But if that is true—this unfortunate train of thought
continues—Christians surely must be unloving and arrogant
toward those who disagree with them: atheists, agnostics,

unbelievers of all kinds, and people of other faiths—perhaps even other Christians who differ on certain points of Christian teaching. Isn't it unloving and arrogant to think that you are right and others are wrong? Today that is widely assumed to be so.

But you only have to restate the question in its generality to know that it is *not* arrogant and unloving merely to believe that you are right about something and that others are wrong. In many contexts it is even vital to human well-being to call attention to errors and mistakes that are being made. It can be the only good and loving thing to do. That negative answer to the question is only slightly obscured, for thoughtful people, by the fact that many who think they are right and others wrong are downright obnoxious as well as arrogant and unloving. Clearly they do not *have* to be that way *just because* they are right or think they are; and when they *are* arrogant and unloving, it results from factors other than the simple conviction that they are right and others wrong.

There have, after all, been many people who were strongly convinced of the rightness of their beliefs, in religious and other matters, *without* being arrogant and unloving. And for very many of those it was precisely upon the basis of assurance about their religious beliefs that they were humble and loving with respect to those who disagreed with them. It could even be unloving and possibly arrogant to *fail* to point out in an appropriate manner where someone is mistaken and taking a wrong path.

LOGICAL EXCLUSIVENESS

Still, there is a certain *logical exclusiveness* built into knowledge as such, and it must be respected. It carries over to whatever religious knowledge there may be. This is due to the fact that knowledge (not mere belief, commitment, sentiment, or tradition) involves *truth*. Truth by its very nature is exclusive in the following sense. If any belief is true, that by itself excludes the truth of any belief contrary or contradictory to it. And this "exclusion" is not a matter of what anyone wants or hopes to be true or false. For example, if "Sue's dress is red" is true, then "Sue's dress is white" and "Sue's dress is not red" are false. It does not matter what anyone may think or want. It is simply a matter of the objective logical relations between the beliefs (or statements or "propositions") involved.

"Pluralism" as a viable human ideal cannot, therefore, be a claim that *all* religious beliefs are true, for many religious beliefs or teachings are contrary or contradictory to others. Nor can it consist in an obligation to *believe* that all religions are equally true, for that would be, as just seen, the obligation to believe some things that are false. No one has a duty to do that. And a belief that all religions are equally true would be psychologically impossible anyway. No one can actually believe that all religions are true—if we are talking about really believing them all and not merely "saying the words." Just try it on a couple of opposed beliefs to see how it goes; and believing a couple of them, if you could do it, would be only a beginning on religious beliefs at large, which are overwhelmingly complicated.

SOMETHING RIGHT ABOUT PLURALISM

Yet there is something right about pluralism, once we get past these "impossible" understandings of it, and it clearly has to do with how we treat those who disagree with us on religious matters, and especially with how we treat other religions and their practitioners. It has to do with having a proper attitude toward them, treating them well, and being appropriately modest and nondogmatic about our own views. If we do know something, that does not mean we are infallible and could not be wrong about it. In explicitly Christian terms "pluralism" has to do with accepting those we don't agree with as our "neighbors" and loving them as we love ourselves—with treating them as we would like to be treated if we were in their place. This distinctively Christian imperative is precisely based upon the knowledge of God, Christ, and right and wrong that we claim as Christ followers. It concerns respect for the sincere efforts of human beings to do what they believe to be good and right.

What we make of this *Christian* imperative depends upon how we understand "pluralism." Standing at the heart of so much social and personal agitation today, pluralism is understood in various ways, and there is considerable confusion about what it means.

A WEAKER FORM OF PLURALISM

Perhaps the weakest form of pluralism is the claim that no one religion captures and conveys *all* truths about God (or a spiritual "beyond"), humankind, and their relationships. This position usually also grants that *many* religions—not necessarily all—teach *some* essential religious truths, if only such "thin" ones as that God exists and that his existence has an important bearing upon human life. Also, some form of prayer and some understanding of sin or impurity, on the one hand, and of redemption ("salvation") or purification, on the other, are present in all major religions. No doubt all also involve some form of "service" or "obedience" to God or the "gods." And something like the Golden Rule is also widespread among religions.

This "pluralism" might well concede that all of these features of religions involve important aspects of truth and goodness and should be respected as such. Those dead set against pluralism in any form would of course deny even that. But disciples of Christ certainly would not have to do so. As we shall see below, outstanding spokespeople for Christ in the Bible itself have been more generous toward other religions than that and have held that the God of the Bible and of Christians deals lovingly and justly with those who fall far short of "getting it all right" in their understanding and in practice.[2] Christians want everything to be exactly what it is. Whatever is good is good, wherever it may show up, and "every generous act of giving, with every perfect gift, is from above, coming down from the Father of lights" (James 1:17). Our intent as followers of Jesus Christ is "to honor everyone" as well as to "love the family of believers" (1 Pet. 2:17).

A STRONGER FORM OF PLURALISM

But things are quite different with a much stronger version of pluralism now commonly held by most people, especially academics. That version is the view that all religions "come out at the same place," that, practically speaking, *which religion you practice makes no difference,* at least not "in the end." In this view, whether you are Islamic, Shinto, or Christian, for example, makes no difference to your prospects for this life or afterward.[3]

It is hard to imagine that *any* sincere adherent of *any* major religion could actually advocate pluralism in this strong sense. It seems to be a position that only those who have no religious identity of their own or who know nothing about the actual practices of the various religions would come up with. But why should the statements of such people be taken seriously? Frankly, they have little or no knowledge of what they are talking about. On the other hand, though some advocates of certain religions talk as if they held this strong version of pluralism, and even seem to take pride in doing so, one cannot help but notice that they continue to hold to their own beliefs and practices, greatly at variance with other religions, and to act as if their beliefs and practices were somehow more important or "better" than those of some other religions. At least "for them." It clearly is not a matter of indifference to them whether *they* continue in their own beliefs and practices or adopt those of other religions with the ease of changing channels on the television.

The usual pluralists in this strong sense hold that it makes no difference to God and to the ultimate destiny of the individual which religion one practices. "Ultimate" issues are taken by them to be out of the range of our knowledge. Completely non-religious "pluralists" even base their view of the sameness of all religions upon the presumed nonexistence of God or an afterlife. In this latter case it is understandable why *they* might be strong pluralists, but if we are right in the foregoing chapters, they are mistaken about God and the afterlife. We do have knowledge of them, and they do exist. Strong pluralism in any case, atheistic or not, is either a blind leap of faith or else it is a position that depends upon a substantial theology—if only a negative one—that must be defended. We return to this point shortly.[4]

DIFFERENCES IN THIS PRESENT LIFE

By contrast, whether the religion one has makes a significant difference *in this life* is a fairly straightforward issue that might be settled by an examination of the "facts of the case." Serious Christians and Jews, for example, do have rather different forms of religious life. They believe and practice quite different things, though as religions go, Christianity and Judaism are probably closer in substance than any other major religions. In comparing religions with regard to this present life, we could overlook mere differences in tastes and styles with respect to things that really don't matter for human well-being—perhaps dress, foods, and other matters that are merely ritualistic. That could be done, but certainly not all religious differences in this life are a matter of taste and style.

It is clear upon very little reflection and with only a superficial knowledge of existing religions that some of them are definitely better for human beings in the present life than others. They are not all equal. Any religion that teaches contempt for people of other faiths, for example, will have serious "this life" effects on human well-being that will keep it from being "equal" to a comparable religion that does not do that. Likewise, a religion that practices human sacrifice would not be "equal" to one that does not. One might, within limits, be "pluralist" with respect to "this life" differences, so long as the differences involved were not too great or only concerned mild disadvantages for the individuals who choose them. But even so, the impact of a religion on the well-being of its practitioners in this present life must be considered when determining whether all religions are to be regarded as equal, and that impact could be a serious one. Clearly, on the other hand, it is *logically possible* that two or more religions as practiced could have approximately the same overall effects for present well-being. That would not mean that *all* do, and they obviously do not. But are the "this life" differences and similarities between religions the ones that really matter for the pluralism issue? Probably not. They matter, but not much for the serious discussion we are engaged in here.

DIFFERENCES BEYOND THIS PRESENT LIFE

By contrast, a pluralism holding that what religion you have makes no difference to *ultimate* issues—to God and the afterlife—assumes much heavier burdens of evidence and knowledge. If pluralism is to be more than a mere shrug of indifference, we must have some reason to think that it is actually true. We would want to know the *basis* of these pluralists' certainty. Do they actually know that differences of religion make no difference to God and will have no effect on what happens after death? What could possibly make anyone think such a thing? It seems highly unlikely on the face of it. And nearly all religions do as a matter of fact hold that one's beliefs and practices make substantial "ultimate" differences.

Of course, we reemphasize, if strong pluralists *know* that there is no God and no continuation of life after death, then there *is* no God and no afterlife and religion will make no difference with respect to them. But the knowledge Christians have, if we are right, places these "transcendental" issues in a new light. The existence of God, the nonphysical source of the physical realm, and the resurrection of Christ and the reality of a spiritual life in Christ undermine the possibility, or at least the plausibility, of a pluralism that holds one's religion makes no ultimate difference. According to Christian teaching it does make a great deal of difference to God what kind of life we lead and what kind of persons we become. And that, in turn, depends upon our relationship to God and Christ. So it seems clear, in the light of Christian knowledge, that one could not justifiably be a pluralist in the strong sense. It matters to "God, the Father almighty" whether we hate our enemy or live sacrificially within our community, whether we accept his provisions for dealing with sin, and so forth. (A similar point is to be made for the teachings of the other major religions as historical realities, not as subjects of academic whimsy.)

MORE TO BE SAID, HOWEVER

But that is by no means the end of the story. The *nature* of the God of the Judeo-Christian tradition and of spiritual life in Christ has important additional implications for the issues surrounding pluralism. In particular, the fact that God is a being whose most basic nature is *agape* love for *all* human beings, *regardless* of their religion or culture, means that he cares for *all* human beings. This lies at the very heart of Christian knowledge. "God so loved the world," we know; and he is "not wanting any to perish" (John 3:16; 2 Pet. 3:9). That is merely the reverse side of biblical monotheism, properly understood, and the heart of the Abrahamic religions. Since he is the God of all, he *cares* for all. He does not sit in splendid isolation demanding that all worship and obey him. He reaches out to them, calls them to himself. His grace is an active principle in his universe. And the one we call "Jesus" is also the Cosmic Christ, present throughout creation and history, inextricably "with" the God of all, throughout time and eternity.

This sense of what Jehovah monotheism means burns through the prophetic consciousness of the Israelites, children of Abraham. For it, the Lord is active among human beings generally. He is their God, whether they know it or not. The prophet Hanani, in the process of rebuking a wayward Jewish king, states: "The eyes of the Lord range throughout the entire earth, to strengthen those whose heart is true to him" (2 Chron. 16:9). God declares himself to all the earth through the universal language of nature (Ps. 19:1–4; cf. Rom. 10:18). He is looking for, actively seeking, those who worship him in spirit and truth (John 4:23–24). The Cosmic Christ is a light that "enlightens everyone" (John 1:9). So we may be sure that God loves all people and is involved with everyone, religious or unreligious, though they may be unaware of it or reject it if they so choose. We are sure of this because of what we *know*, of what we have been put in touch with, as Christ followers.

And now because of the nature of God according to Christian teachings, we are assured that *no one will be treated unfairly by him*. "Shall not the Judge of all the earth do what is just?" (Gen. 18:25). Whatever is good and fair and right will be done by him, to the ultimate satisfaction of everyone. The character of God as love precludes any injustice on his part. He has both the will and the means to see to it that all, Christian or not, are received as they deserve, and indeed much better than they deserve.

Our God is a God of grace, who considers the heart as well as all of the limitations under which human beings labor. In the beautiful words of Psalm 103: "He does not deal with us according to our sins, nor repay us according to our iniquities. . . . As a father has compassion for his children, so the Lord has compassion on those who fear him. For he knows how we were made; he remembers that we are dust" (vv. 10–14). To be sure, our great religious efforts do not impress him. "But," he says, "this is one to whom I will look, to the humble and contrite in spirit, who trembles at my word" (Isa. 66:2). And again, "Hold fast to love and justice, and wait continually for your God" (Hos. 12:6). And yet again, "He has told you, O mortal, what is good; and what does the Lord require of you but to do justice, to love kindness, and to walk humbly with your God?" (Mic. 6:8).

THE "RIGHT HEART" BEFORE GOD

This lesson of the *primacy and sufficiency of the right heart before God* is constantly lost as, in "organized" religion, the merely human side of religious life absorbs the gifts that God has deposited in humanity. It turns them into cultural artifacts expressing human superiority. At no time was this truer than when Jesus walked among us, and there was nothing upon which he laid greater emphasis than returning to the religion of the heart in the kingdom of God. He opened life in the kingdom of God to all kinds of people—especially to those who did not have the "religious goods."

His closest followers as well as his chief enemies really struggled with that, to say the very least. The words of Peter at the beginning of this chapter mark an earthshaking progression in Peter's own understanding and in that of the earliest church. Here Peter had before him a Roman, *a despised Gentile,* to whom an angel had said, "Your prayer has been heard and your alms have been remembered before God" (Acts 10:31). That was before the "Roman" had any knowledge of Jesus. Peter now saw what he should have known already: "God shows no partiality, but *in every nation anyone who fears him and does what is right is acceptable to him*" (vv. 34–35).

In the context of the earliest followers of Christ, the issue was whether people could be acceptable to God if they were not Jews. What we are here concerned with, by contrast, is the question of whether those who are not Christians *by socially recognized standards*—and those standards vary widely from Christian group to group—can be acceptable to God. But the issues are basically the same. It mainly depends, of course, upon how we think of being Jewish or being Christian. In the times of Jesus, Peter, and Paul, being a "good Jew"—an "acceptable" Jew—essentially involved observance of ceremonial law, especially male circumcision, Sabbath observance, food laws, and other rituals. Can one be acceptable to God and not keep these laws distinctive of Jewish religion and culture?

The New Testament Gospels and the book of Acts show that that was a major issue among the earliest students of Jesus, who were all Jews. Paul addresses it head-on in Romans 2. He is there considering the condition of the universal failure and sinfulness of humankind, Jews and Gentiles, confronting the "righteous judgment" of God, who "will repay according to each one's deeds" (Rom. 2:5–6). His main point in this chapter is that whether you are a Jew or a Gentile makes no difference with respect to your ultimate acceptability before God. He says: "To those who by patiently doing good seek for glory and honor and immortality, he will give eternal life; while for those who are self-seeking and who obey not the truth but wickedness, there will be wrath and fury. There will be anguish and distress for everyone who does evil, the Jew first and also the Greek, but glory and honor and peace for everyone who does good, the Jew first and also the Greek" (vv. 7–10). He rhetorically asks: "If those who are uncircumcised keep the requirements of the law, will not their uncircumcision be regarded [by God] as circumcision?" (v. 26). The obvious answer is, "Yes, it will."

"CIRCUMCISION OF THE HEART"

We should note very carefully that Paul is not saying that *everyone* is "okay" with God. He is not a pluralist in *that* sense. Far from it! He is trying to warn precisely those he knows are not "okay." His point is that one's identity as a Jew will not guarantee you are okay with God; you could be a Jew by the "recognized marks" and yet *not* be right with God. He drives this home: "A person is a Jew who is one inwardly, and real circumcision is a matter of the heart—it is spiritual and not literal. Such a person receives praise not from others, but from God" (v. 29).

The same point applies to "Christians" today. Many people who are Christians by certain identifiable *human* standards— say, by baptism, church membership, having "prayed to receive Christ," or regular partaking of the sacraments—still lack the inward "circumcision" of which Paul here speaks. On the other hand, any who lack those recognizable marks, but have the inward heart God looks for is acceptable to God—no matter in what other ways they may or may not be identifiable. *This is the Christian pluralism* of which we here speak. Cornelius, the Roman centurion of Acts 10, is simply a case in point: "He was a devout man who feared God with all his household; he gave alms generously to the people and prayed constantly to God" (v. 2). And God found him!

The old apostle John, the one who, of all New Testament writers, had the longest time to dwell upon Jesus and his revelation of "God, the Father Almighty," puts it all in terms of love: "Everyone who loves is born of God and knows God. Whoever does not love does not know God, for God is love" (1 John 4:7–8). But one must understand that this "love" was and is an incredibly high standard.

Does this mean that these people of love *earned* their salvation? That they *deserved* their acceptance by God? Not at all. It is simply a description of the wideness of God's mercy. The idea that God works with humankind strictly on a basis of merit is a mistake—especially when that merit is defined in human terms, which is the usual case. But the idea that anything and everything is acceptable to God is likewise a mistake. In his goodness and wisdom he responds to the flawed efforts of flawed human-kind to reach him—*by reaching them*. He looks upon the heart: "The Lord does not see as mortals see; they look on the outward appearance, but the Lord looks on the heart" (1 Sam. 16:7). This profound and pervasive prophetic wisdom was stingingly applied to some "righteous persons" of Jesus's day. "You are those who justify yourselves in the sight of others," he said, "but God knows your hearts; for what is prized by human beings is an abomination in the sight of God" (Luke 16:15).

BEYOND RELIGION

So there is a form of genuine pluralism based upon the under-standing of God and of the spiritual life brought to earth in the person and teachings of Jesus Christ. But that pluralism does not say that all religions are the same, or that it is, in *any* case, their religion that makes God reach out to individuals and bring them to him. We recall from Chapter 6 Peter Berger's statement "that the revelation of God in Jesus Christ (which is the object of Christian faith) is something very different from religion."[5] Strangely, perhaps, it is the very focus upon Jesus Christ that nat-urally leads *his* followers into the world of God *beyond religions*. That is where the only justifiable pluralism is to be found. *Beyond religion!* What *this* Christian pluralism says is that, *because* God is who Jesus Christ shows him to be, any person who in God's eyes it seems right for him to accept certainly *will* be accepted by him. *That acceptance will in every case be an act of mercy.* This is a faith in God that excludes boasting of any kind—especially religious boasting—and places everyone on an even footing before God's mercy (Rom. 3:27–31).

Christian pluralism thus concedes that people of "other" re-ligions or no religion at all *may* be "right with God." But from within the resources of its knowledge it insists that, if that is so in a given case, it will not be because the individuals concerned merely profess the beliefs and sustain the practices thought to be essential to recognized members of their particular religious culture—including Christians. It will not be because of their religion. Rather, it will be because their lives are centered on that same love that is expressed in the person and teachings of Jesus and of his people at their best. It will be because God is love.

Many now want to say that if any are *good* Hindus, Christians, or whatever, then they do meet the "love condition" and are "right with God." But unless such a statement is to be treated as a mere definitional statement of "good" Hindus, Christians, or whatever, the facts go against it. It is clearly refuted by cases. There are clearly recognizable "good" persons of those religions who do *not* meet the love condition of Jesus's teachings (or of Paul's description in Rom. 2), including many "good Christians." Religion—of whatever kind—is just not enough. But "everyone who loves [*agape* love] is born of God and knows God. Whoever does not love does not know God, for God is *agape*" (1 John 4:7–8). If you really do have the kind of *agape* love in question, God is living in you and you know God, whatever else may or may not be true of you.

Paul, in his encounters with the pagan world, *never* suggests that God has nothing to do with those who don't have an accurate understanding of him, whether Jewish or Christian. Just the opposite. In the city of Lystra, in what we now call Turkey, people responded to Paul's message and his manifestations of the power of the kingdom of God by trying to worship him and Barnabas. Warding off their efforts, Paul protested that he and Barnabas were just human beings like them. He called upon them to turn away from the familiar Greek gods "to the living God, who made the heaven and the earth and the sea and all that is in them" (Acts 14:15; note the familiar "Creator" theme).

In past generations, Paul told them, that "living" God "allowed all the nations [the Gentiles] to follow their own ways; yet he has not left himself without witness [to them] in doing good—giving you rains from heaven and fruitful seasons, and filling you with food and your hearts with joy" (Acts 14:16–17; see also Matt. 5:45; Rom. 10:18). Note *he*, God, did that. This continues Jesus's theme about God's goodness: "Your Father in the heavens . . . makes his sun rise on the evil and on the good, and sends rain on the righteous and on the unrighteous" (Matt. 5:45). And in Acts 17 Paul indicates that the God he was proclaiming was the one the "Athenians" *worshiped in ignorance,* the "unknown" God: "Therefore what you worship in ignorance, this I proclaim to you" (v. 23, NASB). Human beings do worship God ignorantly, and the God they so worship is not indifferent to them. He does not wait for them to arrive at the perfectly correct views.

SOME ESSENTIAL CLARIFICATIONS

But we frankly admit that it is not easy to understand and accept all of this, and especially from within a religious culture—Jewish or Christian, or any other kind—teaching that God comes to his world through only *that* particular religion. Human beings are addicted to "monopoly" in religion. They want to control access to the divine goods. So a few important clarifications must be made.

First of all, because God is who he is, those who set themselves toward him in an appropriate way—whatever that is, he will decide—will be accepted by him, no matter what. We now take this as established by the nature of God, the Father Almighty. Anyone who understands the God seen in Jesus will hardly be able to say the words that some "deserved" to be saved and yet God did not save them or that someone "missed heaven by a hair." On the other hand, when people are accepted by God, that does not mean that they actually *deserve* or *merit* that acceptance. Anyone who is "saved" will be saved by grace or gift, by the abundant kindness and mercy of the God of love. The bitter truth is that all have sinned and fall far short of what

God had in mind for them. All! That is simply the human condition, whatever one may choose to call it. Any who miss this and fail to particularize it to their own case will very likely not find their way into acceptance before God. They will invariably rely upon their own status or attainments for acceptance with God—perhaps their "good standing" in their religion. As a good rule of thumb, at least, we might say that those who seriously think they really do *deserve* to be accepted by God—think that they are *worthy* of such acceptance—probably are suffering from a severe lack of self-knowledge and had better not count on his acceptance.

"I AM THE WAY, AND THE TRUTH, AND THE LIFE"

A second necessary clarification concerns Jesus's statement, "I am the way, and the truth, and the life. No one comes to the Father except through me" (John 14:6). It is absolutely crucial that we understand this statement correctly, for it has become the central bone of contention with reference to Christian pluralism or exclusivism. Clearly, according to it, *Christ* is exclusive. But is Christianity?

If you take this statement to be saying that no one can "come to the Father" (be accepted by God) without *specific knowledge* of the *historical personage Jesus*—as many people do take it—then of course billions of people, before, during, and after his time on earth are eliminated from all possibility of "coming to the Father" simply by accidents of time and place over which they have no control.[6] (One remembers the traditional doctrine of Limbo, for example, the eternal abode of infants who die unbaptized along with certain others barred from heaven through no fault of their own.) That is surely impossible in a world of which John 3:16 is true.

To relieve any apparent tension between John 3:16 and John 14:6, one has to understand *who is speaking* in the Gospel of John. The one speaking is introduced in the "Prologue" to the Gospel

(1:1–5) as the eternal Word (Logos)—the one who could say, "Before Abraham was, I am" (8:58)—through whom the created universe came into being and who then comes incarnate into that universe to provide a clear way for human beings to return to God. This larger picture of Jesus of Nazareth is one that progressively emerges as the New Testament experience of him moves along. That progression is seen in such passages as Colossians 1–2, Hebrews 1, and Revelation 1, among others.

As he comes toward the end of his Gospel, John explains that he has written it so that readers can understand who Jesus, the historical personage, actually is: "That you may come to believe that Jesus is the Christ, the Son of God, and that through believing you may have life in his name" (20:31). Jesus himself was, obviously, profoundly mysterious to those around him, and he remains so today. That stands out as a major point in the very discussion where he makes his claim to be *the* way to the Father. His closest associates still did not know him (14:7–9), though they knew Jesus of Nazareth. It was not the historical Jesus that Philip did not know (v. 9). Who he was clearly amounted to much more than a carpenter of Nazareth who became a famous rabbi and who was crucified and rose again. He was and is the eternal Word, and whoever comes to the Father comes through the eternal Word. Period.

Where there really is a way to God, where there really is truth about God, where there is genuine life of God, *Christ is there*. That breathtaking thought alone helps us to know better who *Jesus* is and allows us to gain a degree of understanding of the historical personage specifically known to some people on earth as Jesus of Nazareth. Where *Jesus* is known, the question is always: "Who do you say that the Son of Man is?" (Matt. 16:13–16). Of all people, his own followers are the ones who must get the answer to this question right. They must have, and must be sure to present, a "big enough" Jesus.

"NO OTHER NAME UNDER HEAVEN"

But, some will ask, what about the statement by Peter in Acts 4:12: "There is salvation in no one else, for there is no other name under heaven given among mortals by which we must be saved"?

The meaning of any statement is governed by the context in which it occurs. Is this indeed a statement about "coming to the Father," as is the case with John 14:6? Is it a statement about salvation in general or about something else? Is the issue here the same as in John 14? Not at all. You will perhaps recall that Peter and John had just previously brought healing to a man who had been lame from birth; and following Jesus's instructions, they had done so "in the name of Jesus Christ the Nazorean" (Acts 3:6). *That name* is the topic of discussion here. Peter and the disciples were simply following the instructions of Jesus as to how they were to speak and act after his departure. To act "in his name" was to act on his behalf and from his resources. Peter explained to those gathering around him—and around the man now "walking and leaping and praising God" (3:8)—that "by faith in his name, his name itself has made this man strong, whom you see and know" (3:16).

When questioned a little later by the authorities, "By what power or by what name did you do this?" (Acts 4:7), Peter replied, "This man is standing before you in good health by the name of Jesus Christ the Nazorean, whom you crucified, whom God raised from the dead" (4:10). Then comes the statement that mainly concerns us here: "There is salvation in no one else, for there is no other name under heaven given among mortals by which we must be saved" (4:12).

Two things require special attention in understanding what is being said. First of all, the "salvation" spoken of here is "deliverance," which is the generic sense of "salvation" in biblical usage (cf. Exod. 14:13, 1 Sam. 14:45). The specific case of "salvation" and being saved in question here is the deliverance of the lame man from his lifelong affliction. It is *not* the "coming to God" referred to in John 14:6. Of course, the "coming to God" mentioned there would also be a case of deliverance. But the kind of deliverance specifically ascribed to "the name of Jesus Christ the Nazorean" in Acts 4:10–12 is not the "eternal salvation" that John 14:6 ascribes exclusively to the Cosmic Christ, the eternal Logos.

Second, the claim in Acts 4:12 is specifically about "names under heaven given among mortals." There is a clear "exclusiveness" stated here, but it does not concern "coming to God." Rather, it concerns speaking and acting with supernatural power to effect deliverance from the evils and deficiencies that afflict human existence. The claim is that "under heaven, given among mortals," there is no name other than that of "Jesus Christ the Nazorean"—of the historical person, *not* of the Cosmic Christ— that can be effectual in delivering people. It is a claim about the availability of the power of God to meet human need.

This "availability" was a part of the "good news" about the kingdom of God as that good news was lived and preached by the earliest disciples of Jesus. Thus, by the time we get to Acts 8, we find that the *name* was *part* of the gospel Philip was preaching and practicing in Samaria. The Samaritans, "when they believed Philip, who was proclaiming *the good news about the kingdom of God and the name of Jesus Christ,* they were baptized, both men and women" (v. 12). Why was "the name of Jesus Christ" a part of the good news preached? Because it gave human beings access to the kingdom of God and brought that kingdom into play in the course of human deliverance. Peter did not heal the lame man *in the name of* the Logos, the Cosmic Christ, or *agape* love.

Acts 4:12, accordingly, does *not* say that no one can "come to the Father" unless he or she has specific knowledge of the person and work of Jesus of Nazareth. The passage is simply not about that. It is about working in the power of the kingdom of God on behalf of the historical person Jesus Christ. It affirms the *exclusiveness of the name* of Jesus Christ, *among names* on earth, in accessing the power to do such work. Peter's statement is about names "under heaven given among mortals," and as such the name possesses the exclusiveness proper to it.

"CHRISTIAN PLURALISM" AND
THE CHRISTIAN GOSPEL

A third essential clarification is this: the Christian pluralism of which we here speak is *not the Christian gospel*. In fact, Christian pluralism is not really very "good news" at all. It is more like a "loophole" than a gospel. There is little or nothing in it that gives hope to the individual. The Christian gospel, on the other hand, is that by placing your confidence in Jesus as "the One," you can begin now to live in the kingdom of God with him and thus enter into an "eternal living" that continues through life here, right on through what we call death, and forever. *We do not preach Christian pluralism.* We do not tell people to realize *agape* love or to "seek for glory and honor and immortality by patiently doing good," and God "will give eternal life" (Rom. 2:7). That may be something good to know as a possibility, but it is not really *good news,* and it is certainly not the gospel of life in Jesus Christ.

One of the things that tempers enthusiasm for the "message" of Christian pluralism and prevents it from being "good news" is the excruciating difficulty of applying it to a particular case. It does leave a door open, but it does not tell us with any precision where the door is or who actually makes it through that door. It assures us that because God truly is good, merciful, and just, anyone who "deserves" to be saved certainly will be saved. But who does "deserve" it? Do I? Do you? Does Socrates? Does Mahatma Gandhi? Gautama Buddha? Muhammad? Confucius? I am sure I do not. Let others speak for themselves. For my part, I do not want to see anyone "left out." "Let anyone among you who is without sin be the first to throw a stone," as Jesus said on one occasion (John 8:7). But on the other hand, the only way *I* am sure of is the way of relying upon Jesus and following him. No one, I think, is in position to say who does or does not "make the cut" on the basis of "patiently doing good" or of being sufficiently loving, or that anyone actually does so. It is certainly not my place to assure any that they are "in."

In his later years Billy Graham was asked if he believed heaven will be closed to good Jews, Muslims, Buddhists, Hindus, or secular people. He very wisely replied: "Those are decisions only the Lord will make. It would be foolish for me to speculate on who will be there and who won't. . . . I don't want to speculate about all that. I believe the love of God is absolute. He said he gave his son for the whole world, and I think he loves everybody regardless of what label they have."[7] It would, I think, be difficult to improve upon this as a statement about our capacity to judge concerning who will and will not be received by God. (Of course if knowledge of the historical personage, Jesus, is required to be received by God, then the matter is removed from the area of speculation for vast multitudes of people. They are just "out." They do not have the required information.)

The position in which Christ followers find themselves is one of knowing a sure way, an *experiential* way, to God for people today: the way of total reliance upon Jesus Christ, of being his disciple. If what we have said in previous chapters of this book is true, that is a way any sincere persons who learn of Jesus can verify for themselves. God will certainly meet them and accept them in this way, and they can come to know it. Outside of that is an area of uncertainty where the Christian assurance is that God will do whatever is right. *That is the domain of Christian pluralism.*

Possibilities of life with God exist, based in the nature of God as we have come to know it in Christ, but we are not in a position to assure any that those possibilities are or will be actualized in any particular case. We can only hope for the best for others and love them as our neighbors with the love that God has shown to us and to them. In doing so we do not abandon what we know of God in Christ or pretend we do not know it. Christian life is not a charade we indulge in with the thought that it might have some good effect, any more than surgeons or electricians doing their business are engaged in a charade, hoping for an effect. Life following Jesus is real life, based upon real knowledge, undergirding appropriate faith, commitment, and profession.

Christian pluralism is based upon Christian knowledge and upon the Christian faith and character associated with it. Pluralism of *any* kind must have some basis in knowledge and in associated faith and character, or else *it* will be only a *charade*—as, I suspect, it often is today. A crucial question for any outlook, religious or secular, is: What foundation does it lay for pluralism (of which kind?) and for tolerance—more deeply still, for love of neighbor? How does love fit into the "pluralism" picture"? Most important, we must ask of a given outlook: Do you end up with a pluralism or with a "tolerance" without love? And exactly what is the possibility or value of *that*?

FOR DISCUSSION

1. What does "Christian pluralism" mean? Is Christian pluralism possible? Is it biblical?

2. Is it arrogant and unloving to believe you are right and others wrong about some humanly important matter?

3. What kind of "pluralism" is logically and psychologically impossible? What is right about pluralism?

4. What is the "stronger" form of pluralism? What does it mean to say, "The religion one has makes no difference to human life here or hereafter"?

5. Are there obvious differences that various religions make in this present life? Are some religions "better" than others for the issues of "this life"? Give examples.

6. What, exactly, would one have to know to be sure that practicing one religion rather than another makes no difference to God or to what happens after death?

7. In the biblical view, does God "stay in touch" with all human beings of all kinds in all times and places? (Try Acts 14:17; 17:27–28.)

8. *Could* one have a "right heart" in God's eyes, but still not know about the Jewish or Christian relationship to God? What about Cornelius in this respect?

9. What does the biblical idea of "circumcision of the heart" amount to?

10. If God decided to "save" someone who had a "circumcised heart" (Rom. 2:29), would that mean the person *deserved* to be saved? That the person was saved by *works* and *merited* salvation?

11. If a "good" Hindu, Christian, or Muslim were saved, would that be because he or she was a good *Hindu, Christian,* or *Muslim*?

12. Given what you know of God in Christ, do you think that someone might "miss heaven by a hair"?

13. Clearly distinguish Christian pluralism from the Christian gospel.

14. How do you understand the biblical teaching that no one comes to God except through Christ?

EIGHT

Pastors as Teachers of the Nations

I will give you shepherds after my own heart, who will feed you with knowledge and understanding.

JEREMIAH, 3:15

We destroy arguments and every proud obstacle raised up against the knowledge of God, and we take every thought captive to obey Christ.

PAUL, 2 CORINTHIANS 10:4–5

WHO IS TO bring the knowledge that will answer the great life questions that perplex humanity? Who is to teach the world—the "nations," people of all kinds—the *knowledge* that belongs to Christ and his people? In any subject matter the responsibility to teach falls upon those who have the corresponding knowledge. With respect to Christian knowledge, the primary responsibility to teach falls upon those who self-identify as spokespeople for Christ and who perhaps have some leadership position or role in Christian organizations. I shall use the word "pastors" for such people, but the word is here to be taken very broadly; it refers not just to those who hold a position with that title—though it is *especially* for them.

TO ALL THE WORLD

After Jesus had completed all that he intended to do on earth "in the days of his flesh," he left his little group of apprentices or "disciples" to keep on doing what he had been doing while he was with them, but now they were to do it worldwide. He told them to "make disciples of all nations" (all kinds of people) and to "teach them to obey everything" he had commanded them (Matt. 28:18–20). He told them to go to all the world (Greek *kosmon*) and announce the good news to all creation (Mark 16:15). The vision and the task were now cosmic.

How are we to think about this task that Jesus set before his little troop? The greatest danger for us now is that we will think too small, that we will think about it in terms of what we know from contemporary "visible" Christianity—churches, denominations, and so forth—and in terms of the political organization of the current world. Above all, perhaps, we must not think of the task as one of making adherents to a particular brand of Christianity now current. If we do, we will then lose the cosmic viewpoint and see the task only in terms of religious organizations and political realities. Jesus, however, did not send his people out to make Christians or to start churches as we understand them today. He sent them to make *disciples* (students, apprentices) *to him* and, supported by his presence, to teach them *all that he had taught* by word and deed. That is a very different type of enterprise!

The early disciples, like Jesus himself, were totally without "power" in any sense that would be humanly recognized. They were a bunch of first-class "nobodies," and they had no organization behind them. And yet they were to extend his presence and his work (the kingdom of God) throughout the earth. They would be able to do this because of abilities that were not entirely under their control. Those abilities came from the presence of God (the Holy Spirit) with them or "upon" them, just as had been the case with Jesus himself (Acts 10:38). That would enable them, as he said, to "be my witnesses both in Jerusalem, in all Judea and Samaria, and to the ends of the earth" (Acts 1:8). As it turned out, they actually did this, with astonishing effect. Their way of working was simply *speaking* and *being*.

Today we need to understand that "the ends of the earth" includes places like New York, Paris, Tokyo, Cairo, and Moscow, and that the processes of "being his witnesses" are still going on today. Actually they are to go on *here*, wherever "here" is, as well as *there*, wherever "there" is.

WITNESSES MUST SPEAK FROM KNOWLEDGE

We should note that witnesses are, first of all, those who *know* something. They don't just believe something. If you get on the "witness stand" to tell people what you believe or feel strongly about, it will be of no use. That an individual believes something or has been told something is of little interest or importance. By contrast, the witness knows something and makes that knowledge available to others. That is why we have made the issue of *knowledge* the whole point of this book. Jesus said to his covert friend Nicodemus, "We speak of what we know and testify to what we have seen" (John 3:11). That is the pattern for witnesses.

The task of followers of Christ is to know Christ and, in knowing him, to make knowledge of God and of life in God *available* to those around them. That is what responsible people do with knowledge of any important subject. If you have knowledge on any matter of great importance to human beings, it is your duty to make that knowledge available to others. If you know the house is on fire, you must share your knowledge with others. If you know where the bargains are, you tell your friends. If you know how to stop global warming or cure cancer, you have a duty to share that knowledge. Not so of your mere opinions, feelings, or decisions about such matters.

It was in this way that the ancient promise of God to his friend Abraham was to be fulfilled: "In you all of the families of the earth shall be blessed" (Gen. 12:3). The unity of humankind through the unity of God imposes an inescapable demand. The unity of humanity is a genuine moral imperative upon modern humanity that expresses itself in many ways. It is a crying need to which secular humanity tries to find a remedy by social and governmental arrangements of ever increasing scope and intensity. But the unity required is beyond attainment by human beings on their own. It can be achieved only "under God," for it is a unity of love. Otherwise the "moral" imperative of human unity becomes a blood-soaked curse upon the earth at the hands of those who would *force* their way upon others. And "ethnic" distinctions of one kind or another always come into play in coercion to regimented uniformity rather than genial coalescence into organic unity. What has happened in recent decades in Rwanda, Bosnia, and Sudan is not a fluke or some strange thing. It is a natural outcome of what is in the human heart. If you are going to "give peace a chance," you must radically change the human heart. It must be ruled by love under God, founded upon knowledge of God.

The unity of humankind is to be achieved *by witness* to truth in love, co-working with God. In a remarkable continuity with Acts 1:8, Matthew 28:19, Mark 16:15, and Paul's repeated affirmations of human unity under Christ in his letters (Col. 3:11), the prophet Isaiah spoke long ago to Israel for the God of Israel: "It is too light a thing that you should be my servant to raise up the tribes of Jacob and to restore the survivors of Israel; I will give you as a light to the nations, so that my salvation may reach to the end of the earth" (49:6). But this was not to be achieved by political or military power, though the Jews of Jesus's day, including his own apostles, could think only of that. Many today have gone no further in their understanding.

By the force of truth and love alone—spoken and lived—the people of Christ, as they dwell in their part of the earth and move about on earth, "make disciples of all nations," all ethnic groups, all kinds of people. But what that means must be rightly understood if it is to be effectual for good in the way Jesus intended. Most Christians of the Western world today take this directive to "make disciples" to mean doing "missionary work" in *other* parts of the world, especially in "underdeveloped" or "backward" countries. That is how it has been presented to them. Thus they look to "the ends of the earth" from where they stand and forget that the process starts in "Jerusalem and Judea," which in their case is precisely the Western world and its churches. It is right where they live. The "all nations" is *above all* our own "nation." North America, for example, is the primary place for North American Christians to make disciples from the various human groupings, surround them in trinitarian reality, and "teach them to obey everything" Jesus commanded (Matt. 28:19–20). The failure of the American church to do this is very obvious, but to fail here "at home" is to fail the need of the world as a whole.

THE POSITION OF PASTORS

Christian leaders who are spokespeople for Christ—the "pastors," we are calling them here—are to be the teachers of the "nations." They are the ones who, by profession at least, have the knowledge that must be taught to meet desperate human need. Also, they have a social position that depends upon God, not upon human support and approval. Of course, every alternative teaching, from other religions to secular worldviews, that may offer itself to this task must be seriously considered. We should do our best to identify such alternatives and to be thorough and honest in examining what they teach and practice. True spokespeople for Christ need no special advantage and seek none. It is once again—but now on the worldwide stage that comes with "globalization"—a question of the God who answers "by fire" (1 Kings 18:24). Let everyone and everything on the world stage be exactly what it is.

Let all voices be fairly heard. "Their rock is not like our Rock, even our enemies themselves judge this" (Deut. 32:31, NASB) was the ancient testimony, and we cannot do better.

The basic questions upon which life hinges were discussed in Chapter 2. The pastors deal with them. We discussed some of these questions in subsequent chapters: What is real? Does God exist? Does God interact with human life? Who is well-off, and who is a truly good person? Is there a spiritual life in Christ, and how does one enter it? To make "disciples" of Jesus is to bring knowledge of him to people in such a way that they want to know *his* answers to these questions, and the role of pastors is to help them attain the knowledge they seek. Their task is *not* to get people to believe things, to share "Christian" feelings or rituals, to join Christian groups, or to be faithful to familiar Christian traditions—though all of these may have some place. The task of Christian pastors and leaders is to present Christ's answers to the basic questions of life and to bring those answers forward *as* knowledge—primarily to those who are seeking and are open to following him, but also to all who may happen to hear, in the public arenas of a world in desperate need of knowledge of what is real and what is good.

What an audacious thought, some will say, that *pastors*, Christian pastors, should be the teachers of the "nations." This hardly fits their public image or indeed their self-image today. But that is exactly why this chapter had to be written. They are the ones to bring knowledge to answer the four great questions of life. Who else? They have an audience—an audience of people spread, to a greater or lesser degree, throughout the community—and their position in the world as *God's* spokespeople is unique. They deal, if they will, with the questions that frame human worldviews. Answers to those questions provide the orientations of individual lives and whole societies. For good or ill they determine the essential character of all we do, whether we are conscious of them or not. Only Christian pastors are in position to deal with them for the instruction of people generally, and that is the stance *they must choose* to occupy.

SENSUALITY AS A GUIDE TO LIFE

To illustrate, the current guide to reality and what is good in the United States, if not the Western world as a whole, is sensuality or feeling.[1] The worldview answers people now live by are provided by feelings. Desire, not reality and not what is good, rules our world. That is even true for the most part within religion. Most of what Americans do in their religion now is done at the behest of feeling. They judge Christian activities and their own religious condition according to their feelings. The quest for pleasure takes over the house of God. What is good or what is true is no longer the guide.

Our educational institutions now provide no intellectually responsible guidance for worldview answers and often undermine the possibility of any such guidance by spreading a bland skepticism that treats reality as a "human construct." They have, by their own admission, no *knowledge* of good and evil to offer the world. Media and popular arts step in to fill the vacuum of worldview guidance with suggestions and images that reinforce sensuality as the way of life and that appeal to feelings to promote themselves and to get people to buy things they don't need—consumerism as the "good life." Pastors may occasionally protest against this state of things and its impacts upon life, but they do not usually see themselves as bringing *knowledge* to bear against it. They do not forcefully analyze it to the bottom and make unmistakably clear what a disaster it is for humanity. It is doubtful they could understand Peter's admonition to early disciples of Jesus: "As aliens and exiles . . . abstain from the desires of the flesh that wage war against the soul" (1 Pet. 2:11). Wage war against the soul! Certainly that is an accurate picture of the frenetic and fractured lives we live today.

Now, the human world is one in which knowledge is made available to people in general *through institutions* of one kind or another. That is how it must be present as a public resource for living. We had a brief look at this point earlier. What are the responsibilities of pastors in this context? Important things that might very well be known and acted upon by individuals and groups will not be known, and therefore not acted upon, if knowledge concerning them is not made publicly available by groups and institutions that stand before the public for that purpose. The Christian church is a public institution, a familiar social reality. It has a long and well-known, though not well-understood, history and has a massive public presence in the world. It and those who hold positions in it along with all those who would speak for Christ have the responsibility to make knowledge of Christ and the knowledge Christ brings available in the contemporary world. If they do that, they can successfully withstand the tide of sensual culture that now rips apart every moral relationship in life.

BUT THE PASTOR MUST BE ONE WHO KNOWS

Pastors—spokespeople for Christ—must first of all have *knowledge* of the truth and reality they communicate to others. They must do whatever is necessary to gain that knowledge. It is not enough that they be trained to function well within a certain brand of Christianity—to be successful in that context. Their field is real life under God. They must know what knowledge is and who, in general, has it and who doesn't, for that is where the battle lies. They cannot leave this up to secular "experts." It is not enough that pastors identify what the right doctrines are and that they believe them or are committed to them. They must know them to be true and must be living according to the realities they represent. They must have firsthand knowledge ("acquaintance") with the existence of God, the resurrected life of Christ, and the reality and power of love, good and evil, the truth, and the Word of God. They must experience Jesus Christ being "with them always, to the end of the age" (Matt. 28:20) and must be aware of the effects of that.

Pastors must also be careful *not* to claim to know what they do not know and must never pretend to have knowledge they do not have. Foolish claims to know where there is no knowledge have done much to undermine the credibility of teachers for Christ and of Christianity in general. Such false claims have been made for many of the familiar "denominational distinctives" that divide Christian groups today. The peculiarities that define most Christian churches and denominations today do not fall within the domain of knowledge. They are just more or less long-standing traditions and must be treated as such. They may be very good traditions, and, if so, they should be respected. But placing simple traditions in the same category as "mere Christianity" drags the latter away from its proper position as a sober, well-grounded representation of reality. It is then rejected by serious seekers.

Only upon a solid basis of knowledge can spokespeople for Christ have the confidence in what they are saying and doing that allows them to be calm, clear, and courageous facing today's world. It enables them to stand firmly and lovingly in the midst of the constant cultural yammering over who has knowledge and who is right. It is not knowledge, but nervous uncertainty, that makes people dogmatic, close-minded, and hostile—which spokespeople for Christ must never be. Paul wisely said to his young pastor friend, Timothy: "The Lord's servant must not be quarrelsome but kindly to everyone, an apt teacher, patient, correcting opponents with gentleness. God may perhaps grant that they will repent and come to know the truth" (2 Tim. 2:24–25). Only a clear knowledge of reality, of where things really stand, makes possible such an open and gracious attitude.

PASTORS MUST "MAGNIFY THEIR OFFICE"

In today's setting spokespeople for Christ will not easily be granted the status of those who know. That is a status charged with power, and everyone knows it. Resistance to it is in fact a quite recent development in Western history. A hundred years ago, Sunday's sermon or a special lecture by a pastor might be reported on or even printed in Monday's newspaper. The pastor was routinely thought of as one of the most knowledgeable persons in the community. No longer![2] Pastors will have to intelligently claim and defend that position for themselves if they are to hold it in their own eyes and in the eyes of others. They must make a point of that, though not in a flamboyant or overbearing way. It must be done intelligently, gently, and modestly. But persistently. Each one must say as Paul said of himself: "I magnify my office" (Rom. 11:13, KJV); that is, "I make much over the greatness of the work I do."

In conjunction with that, pastors must *present* the fundamental points of basic Christianity *as* knowledge, and as knowledge that is testable and available to anyone who truly wants to know. They must not only possess knowledge of those points, but they must make sure to present what they teach *as* knowledge—knowledge that can be verified by individuals who have an interest and will invest the time and effort required to do so. *They will have to state this explicitly and repeatedly* and deal with the public pressures of a world that goes against it. And they must stand ready to help people through the steps that will lead them to genuine knowledge. They must work for people's *insight*, not just train them to jump through official hoops dictated by the particular group or to "place their hands over their eyes and believe."

An incident in the life of Jesus is instructive on this point. As he taught in the temple on one occasion, his hearers were amazed—and a little offended—at how much he knew and with what confidence he spoke. Everyone was aware that he had not had what we might call a "formal education." He did not speak like a "scholar" (Matt. 7:28–29). This was brought up as a challenge to him and to what he was saying. Could he really know what he was talking about? Could he be trusted? His response was that what he taught came to him from God, not through human education. But he did not burden his hearers with the demand to "just believe." No, he told them, "Anyone who resolves to do the will of God will know whether the teaching is from God or whether I am speaking on my own" (John 7:17).

This was the confidence of Jesus, and it must be the confidence of pastors. They present basic truths as knowledge from God, with confidence that those truths can be verified by any who want to do God's will. We can be confident that to such persons a way will be opened to know the truths we teach. That knowledge of those truths is "from God" does not mean that it bypasses ordinary human faculties. The proper use of those faculties—no doubt "under God"—will bring people to knowledge of the basic truths we represent.

But we must squarely face the fact that in today's world all the presumptions are against this, not least among professing Christians themselves. It is therefore crucial for the success of Christ's cause and the good of humanity that those who speak now for Christ *consciously and intentionally* stand as those who have *knowledge* of the basic truths and realities of the way of Christ. Because of the pressures of modern thought and contemporary life, they are likely not to do this. Indeed, it is rarely done, and that does much to explain the weakness of Christian understanding, commitment, behavior, and witness today.

Pastors now are mistakenly seen, and perhaps even see themselves, as teaching *what Christians are supposed to believe* (perhaps what we had *better* believe), not what is known and what can be known through fair inquiry. And upon that supposition their job is taken to be to get hearers to believe it—or at least to *commit* to it, or minimally to *profess* it. Thus knowledge along with belief, commitment, and profession founded on knowledge are bypassed. We are left with "converts" whose "faith" does not govern their lives and whose "Christianity" may be only social conformity with a tinge of fear. Pastors then must exhaust themselves trying to get these people do things they "ought" to do, but have no serious vision or motivation for. Religion is then experienced by everyone involved as a drag on life. "Getting people to do things for the church" becomes a pastor's or leader's de facto job description. Boredom, burnout, and dropout are at hand.

PAUL'S WAY

By contrast, presenting knowledge as knowledge, spokespeople for Christ do not try to manipulate the hearers' feelings or actions in any way. They can lay down the burden of getting people to do things. They know that passion comes from reality and simply do their best to help willing hearers understand and come to know the reality and goodness of life in the kingdom of God with Jesus. Any result beyond this they leave to the influence of the Word of God speaking in the heart and to the work of the Holy Spirit in and around the people involved.

The apostle Paul often speaks in his letters of how he worked "with Christ" to bring people to God—with amazing success. He simply spoke plainly to them, without manipulative devices of any kind, relying on the Spirit of God to give his words the effect they should have. Thus his hearers themselves became "a letter of Christ, prepared by us, written not with ink but with the Spirit of the living God, not on tablets of stone but on tablets of human hearts. Such is the confidence we have through Christ toward God" (2 Cor. 3:3–4).

This "confidence" makes pastors hopeful and transparent. Paul continues: "Therefore, since it is by God's mercy that we are engaged in this ministry, we do not lose heart. We have renounced the shameful things that one hides; we refuse to practice cunning or to falsify God's word; but by the open statement of the truth we commend ourselves to the conscience of everyone in the sight of God" (2 Cor. 4:1–2).

John Wood Oman wrote these words on how spokespeople for Christ proceed:

> There is only one right way of asking men to believe, which is to put before them what they ought to believe because it is true; and there is only one right way of persuading, which is to present what is true in such a way that nothing will prevent it from being seen except the desire to abide in darkness; and there is only one further way of helping them, which is to point out what they are cherishing that is opposed to faith. When all this has been done, it is still necessary to recognize that faith is God's gift, not our handiwork, of His manifestation of the truth by life, not of our demonstration by argument or of our impressing by eloquence; and that even He is willing to fail till He can have the only success love could value—personal acceptance of the truth simply because it is seen to be true.[3]

FAIRNESS TO ALTERNATE "ANSWERS"

Further, as briefly indicated above, spokespeople for Christ must be careful to understand and properly evaluate "answers" to the main life questions that come from other sources and are contrary to "mere Christianity" or the basic teachings of Christ. Complete fairness, thoroughness, and openness need to govern this enterprise, because these are traits of those concerned to arrive at knowledge. We need to be very conscious of the three contemporary "stories," or worldviews, mentioned at the end of Chapter 2 as being influential today. We need to clearly and fairly know why the "answers" provided, explicitly or implicitly, by the "naturalistic" and the "nirvana" stories are inadequate as knowledge for human life.

These "stories" and other sources of answers to life's great questions must be accurately understood and fairly and graciously represented if they are to be appropriately dealt with in "teaching the nations." The aim is not to prove "we" are right. No unfair advantage should be attempted. Smallness of mind and ill will are to be totally excluded. If we are operating from genuine knowledge and "with Christ," we can afford to be generous. Of course, not all pastors can carry through with all of this project on their own; but they can, if they will, know other spokespeople who do carry it through. Pastors must stand in a spiritual and intellectual community, where responsibilities are effectively shared. Communication among them must have high priority. Pastors must speak from an effectual community of disciples.

"CHRISTIAN" HIGHER EDUCATION

A great responsibility with regard to that community falls upon Christian institutions of higher education—colleges, universities, and seminaries. They are at the center of the battle for the human mind and spirit. They are not just centers of learning— they train pastors. They claim to teach, to inquire, and to bring Christian knowledge, and to do so as disciples of Jesus Christ. Yet, with almost no exception, they today teach *as knowledge* exactly what secular institutions teach. Their courses in the subject areas usually do not differ in knowledge content from courses in other schools so far as testable (gradable) content is concerned. Most important, they do not present the basic points of the Christian faith as constituting a body of Christian knowledge that Christians have and non-Christian institutions do not have. There are various reasons why this is so, but it *is* so, and that must be acknowledged if we are to deal honestly with where we now stand as pastors and leaders. I realize that what I am saying here is very radical and I would be pleased to be shown that it is false.

Not too long ago, even "state" schools presented basic Christian truths as a body of necessary knowledge. This was because the basic teachings of Christianity were generally regarded as essential knowledge vital to life. A well-educated person with expectation of leadership and social responsibility would be expected to know them and act according to them.[4] Of course, this is no longer true, and there are reasons why a change had to occur. But could there be any good reason why *explicitly Christian* institutions of higher education would not carry on in that tradition of teaching the Christian answers *as* knowledge?

Upon those in *Christian* higher education, more than upon anyone else, there now falls the burden of "teaching all nations" the *knowledge* of God and his kingdom that Christ brings to humanity. They must no longer think of Christ, their professed Lord, as an airhead who stands haplessly before people with PhDs. Individuals from all over the world come to "Christian" institutions of higher education in America to receive training. However, they now by and large receive the clear impression that Christianity is only a "leap" of faith or an irrational "impact" of some kind—even an emotional condition—or just one of many "traditions" within "diversity." This is the tone that Christian faculty pick up as secular dogma in the programs where they receive their higher degrees. They are in danger of being permanently paralyzed by it. One of the greatest challenges facing spokespeople for Christ in higher education is how to understand the relation of the basic things they believe as Christians to their responsibility for knowledge in their professional field.

One thing is for sure. Until institutions of Christian higher education and their faculties break out of a posture that holds genuine knowledge to be secular, and until they carry out their task of developing and conveying distinctively Christian knowledge—in the free, open, and rational manner that characterizes the life of the mind and of scholarship at its ideal best—those institutions will, despite all appearances, be a primary *hindrance* to the "Jesus project" on earth. They will leave the impression, now almost universally held, that being a follower of Jesus Christ is simply a matter of what one believes and feels, a "personal preference" as is now said, not something essentially involving knowledge of truth and of a reality that everyone must come to terms with.

No "integration of faith and learning"—so often spoken of in Christian academic circles—is possible under the weight of that smothering impression, because "faith" and "learning" (knowledge) are taken under it to fall into different life categories, where no intellectually coherent contact is possible. Faith and learning may happen to exist in the same person, but asking about the *integration* of faith and knowledge under current assumptions is a bit like asking whether more people live in the city or in the winter. You might be able to respond to it somehow, but there is something wrong with the question.[5] Only when "faith" is understood to deal with things that can also be known, only when faith is at home with knowledge, does the project of integrating "faith and learning" have a manageable sense.

DISCIPLES ARE FOR THE WORLD GOD SO LOVES

One final point about pastors as teachers of the "nations." Pastors are sent to make disciples of Jesus, apprentices to Jesus in kingdom living. Life is primarily devoted to work. All legitimate work is devoted to the creation of value, of what is good to a lesser or greater degree. That was God's plan. He not only creates; he creates creators—you and me. One of the saddest things in human life is the desecration of work in a loveless world. Discipleship to Jesus, properly guided by pastors, enables individuals to find in their work a divine calling and see the hand of God in their efforts to create what is good and to serve others in love.

Pastors for Christ teach the "nations" by declaring the presence of the kingdom everywhere and by pointing out the availability of eternal life now in the kingdom of God. We have only to rely upon Jesus Christ as *the One totally in charge*. The kingdom is for whole life and for all of life. Jesus is not just a sacrificial lamb whose death gets us off the hook of our guilt. He is also the reigning Lord of all. The result of *this* declaration, by word and example, will be the people who emerge into discipleship to him. There will always be such people where the gospel of the kingdom is spoken and lived. Pastors *primarily* work with them, teaching them how to be God's men and women in the places they work and live. They are the ones who have decided to learn from Jesus how to lead their life—all of it, their actual existence—in the kingdom of God. Practically, that means they are becoming, in the fellowship of disciples, people who routinely and easily do in all real-life circumstances the kinds of things Jesus did and said. "We are what he has made us, created in Christ Jesus for good works, which God prepared beforehand to be our way of life" (Eph. 2:10).

Therefore the focus of discipleship to Christ is not the church, but the world. If it is focused on the church, it will stagnate and leave most people at dead end, for their life is not the church. Discipleship is *for the sake of the world,* not for the sake of the church. It is carried out in those situations where people spend their life. Above all, the "world" is *work,* the realm of creativity for which human beings were created according to Genesis 1:26. For most people that means our job—our "position" if you like.[6] Unfortunately, "discipleship" as Christian groups now teach and practice it, where they do so at all, consists mainly of "special" activities of various kinds, religiously characterized, motivated, and organized. But we recall Peter Berger's lifesaving words: "The revelation of God in Jesus Christ . . . is something very different from religion." It concerns our work in life. It is this that God redeems, and with it our life, and with it our souls.

THE CHURCH IS NOT THE CENTRAL
FOCUS OF DISCIPLESHIP

The revelation of God in Jesus Christ is a life from God—"from above," from "the heavens" always near. That life informs and makes eternal all that we do, with divine direction and empowerment. "Pastors" train disciples for work in the world. Thus our "job" is turned into calling or vocation. Given this understanding of what human life was meant to be, Paul writes to the Colossian disciples: "Whatever your task, put yourselves into it, as done for the Lord and not for your masters, since you know that from the Lord you will receive the inheritance as your reward; you serve the Lord Christ" (Col. 3:22–24). All day every day I am working for Jesus Christ. It is what *he* is doing that carries me. He is my boss and my paymaster. The forces of evil are stymied wherever I am as I consciously do my work with him.

It will come as a shock to many to think that Jesus did not tell his followers to make Christians or start churches, as we automatically think of Christians and churches today. He certainly knew there would be churches in his special sense of "ones called out" from the merely human order. These would be people who have a new and unique standing among human beings. In fact they would be a new and unique version of humanity (Eph. 2:15). They would be *in* this world, but not *of* it. The sources of their life would not be just the "natural" order of things, but God and his kingdom. Jesus said he was in charge of *this* church and would bring it to pass against all possible opposition from evil ("the gates of Hades," Matt. 16:17–19). There would be local groups of such unique people, of course; and there would also be one great "church," the *body* of Christ, consisting of all his followers throughout time and space. As disciples in local settings people would be drawn together in the natural connections of life, right where they are, in fellowship with the Father, the Son, and the Holy Spirit.

"Pastors," then, are the ones who guide disciples into *their place in their world* and show them how to "exercise dominion in life through the one man, Christ Jesus" (Rom. 5:17). Real life, "ordinary" life, is the place of disciples and the place of discipleship. There disciples "reign" in the office, laboratory, farm, the schoolroom as well as in media, sports, the fine arts, and so forth. They reign for what is good in the home, the community, and in voluntary and involuntary associations of all kinds, even up to international organizations and relations. They effectively care for the goods of human life that come under their care and influence. "The fruit of the light is found in all that is good and right and true" (Eph. 5:9). Special "church" activities involve the fellowship of disciples in worship, teaching, learning, and caring for one another. Those activities constitute a school of love. But all of that is for the creative life of individuals in their world and their work. There they will form and exercise the character that they will carry forward in eternity. "Divine service" is not a *church* service, though it might include that. Divine service is life. It is in the world, in daily business of whatever level and importance, that there unfolds, in Paula Houston's wonderful phrase, "the great adventure that was once Christianity."[7] It can be so for every one of us.

The most important thing that is happening in your community is what is happening there under the administration of true pastors for Christ. If you, as a pastor, do not believe that, then you do not understand the dignity of what you are supposed to be doing. Whatever your situation, there is nothing more important on earth than to dwell in the knowledge of Christ and to bring that knowledge to others.

FOR DISCUSSION

1. Who has the responsibility of bringing Christian knowledge to the "nations"?

2. What was the project Jesus left for his disciples to carry out? How inclusive was it? How long was it to last?

3. What is required of a witness in court? In life? Will an expression of your beliefs and feelings be enough?

4. How is the moral unity of humankind under God to be achieved? World government? Education? Christian witness under "pastors"?

5. Why is it that "pastors" have the unique role of teaching the "nations"—people of all kinds the world around?

6. Is sensuality, the worship of feeling, pleasure, and desire, the practical guide to life in our culture? Would careful readers of the New Testament be surprised at where we are today? (See Rom. 1:21–32; Eph. 4:17–22; 2 Tim. 3:1–7.)

7. What happens if "pastors" do not actually *have knowledge* of the Christian answers to the four basic questions of life? Do they "just believe"?

8. How are pastors to "magnify their office"?

9. What would be involved in presenting the Christian answers to the world *as* knowledge?

10. What was Paul's confidence in bringing knowledge of Christ to the "nations"?

11. How does Christian "higher education" fit into the picture of "teaching the nations"? What is its primary challenge today?

12. Where is the focus of discipleship to Christ, in the church or in the world? What are pastors training disciples to do, preparing the "nations" for? Start with their job. Go on to their responsibilities under Genesis 1:26.

If you indeed cry out for insight,
And raise your voice for understanding;
If you seek it like silver,
And search for it as for hidden treasures—
Then you will understand the fear of the Lord
And find the knowledge of God.
PROVERBS 2:3–5

Notes

INTRODUCTION

1. J. E. Lesslie Newbigin, *A Faith for This One World* (London: SCM, 1961), p. 30.
2. *Meno*, Stephanus pagination 98.
3. Seduced by a misunderstanding of the Pauline and Protestant teaching that faith is some sort of miracle because it is a gift of God, writers as widely divergent as David Hume and Søren Kierkegaard have wildly misconstrued Christian faith to be something opposed to knowledge. That faith is a gift does not mean it is not essentially environed in knowledge, much less that it is opposed to it. Sloppy thinking on such matters undergirds entire cultural agendas and historical epochs. Its effects on our day are nothing short of catastrophic.
4. Evelyn Waugh, *Brideshead Revisited* (Boston: Little, Brown, 1946), pp. 85–86. Quoted in my *The Divine Conspiracy* (San Francisco: HarperSanFrancisco, 1998), p. 92.
5. Dr. William B. Provine, professor of Biological Sciences, Cornell University, cited in Roger Patterson, *Evolution Exposed* (Hebron, KY: Answers in Genesis, 2006), p. 82. See Provine, W. B., *Origins Research* 16 (1), 1994, p. 9. These kinds of sweeping, unscientific statements, made in the name of "science," have become commonplace in our academic culture during the last two centuries. We have recently had a massive outbreak of such statements, but there is a steady stream of them reaching from Ludwig Büchner's *Force and Matter* (first German edition 1855; several English editions) to the present.
6. Aristotle, *On the Parts of Animals*, bk. 1, chap. 1.
7. C. S. Lewis, *The Screwtape Letters* (New York: Macmillan, 1962), first "letter."

8. The flight to Eastern religions during the 1950s and 1960s was a flight from a religion (standard Christianity) that did not offer knowledge to ones that did—did *offer* it.

9. More on this important point below. Texts used to introduce the subject of religion in university courses routinely *make no mention* of the possibility that religion arises in human life out of genuine divine-human interactions.

10. C. S. Lewis, *Mere Christianity* (New York: Macmillan, 1956), p. 61.

CHAPTER 1: CAN FAITH EVER BE KNOWLEDGE?

1. For a deeper engagement with issues involving faith and knowledge than we can undertake here, excellent resources are John Hick, *Faith and Knowledge,* 2d ed. (Ithaca, NY: Cornell University Press, 1966) and D. M. Baillie, *Faith in God,* new ed. (London: Faber and Faber, 1964). For a deeper philosophical study, see James Kellenberger, *Religious Discovery, Faith, and Knowledge* (Englewood Cliffs, NJ: Prentice-Hall, 1972).

2. For a beginning, see, e.g., Exod. 8:10; 9:14; 29:44–46; Ezek. 37:27–28; Joel 3:17.

3. Alvin Plantinga, "Rationality and Religious Belief," in David Shatz, ed., *Philosophy and Faith: A Philosophy of Religion Reader* (New York: McGraw Hill, 2002), p. 443.

4. For a simple introduction, see David Friedrich Strauss, *The Old Faith and the New* (1872; Amherst, NY: Prometheus, 1997). The general approach of liberal theology lives on today in the works of most members of the Jesus Seminar, for example, and of others such as Bishop John Shelby Spong. Generally speaking, antisupernaturalism and opposition to the miraculous characterize this tendency and are utilized as a premise to purge most of the tenets of historical Christianity from biblical texts, leaving now only "social ethics."

5. This is in fact a very old strand of Christian thought, most famously associated with Tertullian and, much later, with Søren Kierkegaard.

6. Elton Trueblood, *The Predicament of Modern Man* (New York: Harper & Row, 1944) p. 52.

7. Arthur Schlesinger Jr., representative of a whole army of the intellectual elite, claimed that "only those who believe in absolute values can achieve the conviction of infallibility which permits tyranny and murder; and . . . if there is anything from which the pragmatist flinches, it is the hypostatization of his own tentative, fragmentary, and incomplete views into dogmatic fanaticism" ("Whittaker Chambers and His Witness," *Saturday Review,* May 26, 1952, p. 41). Thanks to Hyrum S. Lewis for this reference. This statement embodies another overriding myth of the current intellectual world. It makes many false assumptions that cannot be examined here. Suffice it to say it locates evil in the wrong place.

8. Allan Bloom points this out in his *The Closing of the American Mind* (New York: Simon and Schuster, 1987).

9. Jacob Bronowski, *The Ascent of Man* (Boston: Little, Brown, 1973), p. 374.

10. Secular humanism, in its "official documents" and not just in the accusations of its critics, explicitly owns the status of a religion or of being religious in its nature. See *The Humanist Manifestos I and II*, ed. Paul Kurtz (Amherst, NY: Prometheus, 1973).

11. Broadcast May 19, 2007, 12–1 p.m. Pacific time.

12. *The Harvard Crimson*, online edition, October 27, 2006.

13. This is not unknown among scientists themselves. See the excellent article by Herman Daly, "Feynman's Unanswered Question," *Philosophy and Public Policy Quarterly* 26 (Winter/Spring 2006): 13–17. Richard Feynman is one of the most respected scientists of the last half century, and he rightly sees that the scientific understanding of nature yields no guidance for human life, including what to do with the knowledge science offers.

14. See Augustine's *Sermon 117* and *Sermon 126*.

15. J. I. Packer, *Knowing God* (Downers Grove, IL: InterVarsity, 1973), p. 19. Packer's book is a straightforward explanation of the main properties or attributes of God, very much on the order of works such as Stephen Charnock's (1628–80) *The Existence and Attributes of God*, though far more merciful in style. Our intent here is rather different from these straightforward treatments and from other more devotional works such as A. W. Tozer's *Knowledge of the Holy*—though we are in total sympathy with them. We want to try to help readers with problems that arise in the modern world from the very idea of there being knowledge of God, and especially those problems that arise out of the context of contemporary education and professional life. Many years ago a publishing arm of the Anglican Church could with no hesitation or resistance call itself "The Society for the Propagation of Christian Knowledge" (S.P.C.K). Now the initials are all that most people know of it, if that. Just as well, perhaps. We are now in a different world, where "Christian knowledge" looks to many people like an oxymoron or a self-contradiction. *That* is the world we have to deal with here.

CHAPTER 2: EXACTLY HOW WE PERISH FOR LACK OF KNOWLEDGE

1. This famous statement, that the just shall live by faith, originates in the writings of the Jewish prophet Habakkuk (2:4). The context makes it clear that the faith he has in mind arises within a setting of firm knowledge of God and of his ways of working among human beings.

2. Aristotle, *Metaphysics*, opening words.

3. Plato, *Meno*, standard pagination pp. 77–78.

4. The idea of "worldview" is of crucial importance in understanding how faith and knowledge work in life. We cannot develop it at length here, but the following sources will provide a thorough understanding of it: Arthur F. Holmes, *Contours of a World View* (Grand Rapids, MI: Eerdmans, 1983); James W. Sire, *Naming the Elephant: Worldview as a Concept* (Downers Grove, IL: InterVarsity, 2004); David K. Naugle, *Worldview: The History of a Concept* (Grand Rapids, MI: Eerdmans, 2002). J. P. Moreland's *Kingdom Triangle* (Grand Rapids, MI: Zondervan, 2007) is an especially valuable treatment of how worldview affects the moral and spiritual life.

5. People love darkness, as Jesus points out in John 3:19, because their deeds are evil. This is a familiar fact of life. Bernard Lonergan calls this condition "scotosis," from the Greek word for "darkness." See his *Insight* (London: Longmans, Green, 1957), p. 191.

6. This is the assumption behind Satan's question to God concerning Job: "Does Job fear God for nothing?" (1:9–11). It turned out Job actually *did* fear God for nothing in the way of reward. He was no idolater.

7. The address given at the dedication of Mudd Hall of Philosophy at the University of Southern California was framed around this story. *The Personalist: Supplement,* July 1930, published by the University of Southern California, Los Angeles, California.

8. See "The Curse of Self-Esteem: What's Wrong with the Feel-Good Movement," *Newsweek,* February 17, 1992, pp. 46–52.

9. Over a period of decades in the twentieth century, the willingness to speak seriously of persons as *good* or *bad* has disappeared from the academic world and from social circles thought to be "enlightened." A very good ethical theorist memorialized the passing of this language in 1921. In defining his subject matter he remarks: "We all know more or less what a moral judgment is, and we are all, of course, constantly making them. So-and-so is a good (or a bad) man, such-and-such an action is right (or wrong), are two types of the commonest forms of them." And to this statement he attaches a footnote: "In ordinary conversation as a matter of fact, we are rather inclined to avoid the use of these terms for fear of laying ourselves open to a suspicion of priggishness. Most people would prefer to use some slang expression: 'So-and-so is a decent fellow.' 'That's a rotten thing to do.' But of course these are just as much moral judgments, and mean exactly the same thing" (G. C. Field, *Moral Theory: An Introduction to Ethics* [London: Methuen, 1932], p. 2).

But, "of course," they do *not* mean exactly the same thing, and it is remarkable that this usually very careful writer should say so. Specifically, being "decent" and being "good" diverge radically. If told that someone is a decent person, one might still wonder: "But is she a really *good* person, or just not particularly bad?" There is a great difference. To say someone is "decent" may be only to damn them with faint praise. In fact, what had emerged at this point in the history of the "enlightened" world was unwillingness to engage in moral judgments of any personal depth and seriousness, along with the sentiment that anyone who did so was a "prig," that is, someone who, a dictionary says, "offends or irritates by observance of proprieties in a pointed manner or to an obnoxious degree." What had actually happened was a cataclysmic shift in the moral *Zeitgeist* of the Western world. (A "prig" in its older meaning is a tinker or a petty thief.) On these matters, see Mary Midgley's invaluable *Can't We Make Moral Judgments?* (New York: St. Martin's, 1991).

10. This was very well understood and portrayed by earlier scholars such as T. H. Green, Bernard Bosanquet, and Christopher Dawson; more recently, by Jürgen Habermas.

11. Plato, *Apology,* Stephanus Pagination 25. The Chinese teacher Mo Ti (fourth century BCE) also taught that mutual love would eliminate all moral harm between people. The question of how you get people to be like that remains the unsolved problem of the contemporary world.

12. There is, I think, a pervasive recognition of this, or at least an enduring suspicion, among the leaders of twentieth-century thought. One of the clearest and most forceful statements is by Edmund Husserl in his *The Crisis of European Sciences and Transcendental Phenomenology* (Evanston, IL: Northwestern University Press, 1970); see esp. §2, pp. 5–7.

13. Anthony Kronman, "Colleges Ignore Life's Biggest Questions, and We All Pay the Price," *New York Times,* September 16, 2007. Also see his book *Education's End: Why Our Colleges and Universities Have Given Up on the Meaning of Life* (New Haven, CT: Yale University Press, 2007).

14. Daniel Yankelovich, "Ferment and Change in Higher Education in 2015," *Chronicle of Higher Education* 52, iss. 14 (November 26, 2005): B6. See the fascinating take on the problem in Herman E. Daly, "Feynman's Unanswered Question," *Philosophy and Public Policy Quarterly* 26 (Winter/Spring 2006): 13–17.

15. Few people today realize how novel and unfounded are these current understandings. Well into the twentieth century a "science" was simply a systematically organized body of knowledge. This was the established usage from antiquity. The transformation of the older usage into the one we have today, in lockstep with progress in the professionalization and secularization of the academic fields, is a fascinating study in the "sociology of knowledge."

16. Owen Flanagan, *The Problem of the Soul* (New York: Basic Books, 2002), p. 40.

17. The members of the Philosophy Department at Princeton, some decades ago, were queried by the Astronomy Department as to whether they would like to hear a presentation from a visiting scholar on "The Philosophy of

an Astronomer." They smartly replied by asking if the Astronomy Department would like to hear a presentation on "The Astronomy of a Philosopher." That ended the exchange.

18. John Wesley, a remarkably deep and clear thinker, held that four sources of information and truth should be brought systematically to bear in determining religious/Christian truth: scripture, tradition, reason, and experience. See Albert C. Outler's interpretation, "The Wesleyan Quadrilateral—In John Wesley," available online from the Wesley Center for Applied Theology at Northwest Nazarene University (Nampa, ID 83686).

19. For a more adequate depiction of how knowledge actually works in real life, see Esther Meek, *Longing to Know: The Philosophy of Knowledge for Ordinary People* (Grand Rapids, MI: Brazos, 2003) and Robert Goodman and Walter Fisher, *Rethinking Knowledge: Reflections Across the Disciplines* (Albany: State University of New York, 1995).

20. For a rather "official" statement of the secularist view, see *The Humanist Manifestos I and II,* ed. Paul Kurtz (Amherst, NY: Prometheus, 1973).

CHAPTER 3: HOW MORAL KNOWLEDGE DISAPPEARED

1. Jürgen Habermas, *Time of Transitions* (Cambridge: Polity Press, 2006), pp. 150–51. Until the latter half of the twentieth century, the influence of Christianity went without saying, though it was often said. *What If Jesus Had Never Been Born?* by D. James Kennedy and Jerry Newcombe (Nashville, TN: Thomas Nelson, 1994), provides a popular but effectual survey of the impact of Jesus and his teachings upon human history, especially in the "West." For an earlier statement, from before the "reaction" took over, see Bernard Bosanquet, *The Civilization of Christendom, and Other Studies* (London: S. Sonnenschien, 1893). Also Glenn Tinder, "Can We Be Good Without God?" *Atlantic Monthly,* December 1989, pp. 69–85.

2. The increasing tendency to think of moral values simply as religious values fortifies this understanding, for religion itself is thought to be doubly removed from knowledge of reality. A widely used harassment prevention program defines religion: "Religion is broadly defined as an individual's moral or ethical system of belief." Then, of course, there will be no nonreligious persons. This same program says: "Gender, though sometimes used interchangeably with sex, is best defined as an individual's internal, personal sense of being a man, a woman, a transgender person or a different gender entirely." One of course understands, in today's world, what this is all about, but with respect to reality (What's that?), it is intellectually appalling. "A different gender entirely" is put in just in case "we" decide to have yet another one. Gender is to be a matter of how one thinks and feels about oneself. One must be free to *decide* one's gender. (The program is "Sexual Harassment Prevention Training with Unlawful Harassment

Supplement," required of all faculty and staff by the University of Southern California in 2007.)

3. Thus arises a new form of the "tyranny of the *minority*," namely, of those who are in position and have the resources to work the existing legal and political system to override the will and the good of the people generally to get what they want. As the Bible and Plato wisely understood, democracy is no guarantee against tyranny, for "the people" are highly manipulable. Tyranny in many forms lurks about it. Hitler was elected by "The People."

4. Joseph Butler, Immanuel Kant, and F. H. Bradley, among many other great ethical thinkers, have emphasized the accessibility of moral knowledge to plain people.

5. Cf. Alasdair MacIntyre, "A Disquieting Suggestion," in his *After Virtue*, 2d ed. (Notre Dame, IN: University of Notre Dame Press, 1984), pp. 1–5. For reasons that cannot be gone into here, I disagree strongly with this brilliant thinker on how to understand the phenomenon of the loss of moral knowledge. He is right on, however, in his recognition and portrayal of the *fact*.

6. A brilliant and widely popular presentation of this point of view, from a hundred years ago, was by Henry Drummond. See, for example, his *The Greatest Thing in the World* (London: Collins, 1953). For a more academic statement, see G. H. Palmer, *The Field of Ethics* (Boston: Houghton Mifflin, 1901), pp. 210–13.

7. An invaluable resource for pursuing this point is George Marsden, *The Soul of the American University* (New York: Oxford University Press, 1994). This should be followed by study of Julie A. Reuben, *The Making of the Modern University* (Chicago: Chicago University Press, 1996). There is by now a veritable sea of scholarly literature establishing and explaining this point.

8. "Folkways" is a term made popular by William Graham Sumner, a major figure in the transition we are dealing with. See his *Folkways* (Boston: Ginn, 1906). He taught at Yale from 1866 to 1909. According to him, to say that an action is "right" just means that it conforms to the "folkways" of the agent's cultural group. See also Edward Westermarck, *Ethical Relativity* (Paterson, NJ: Littlefield, Adams, 1960). The writings of Margaret Mead and Ruth Benedict did most to popularize this view. Their "scholarship" has, more recently, come under rather severe criticism from the point of view of valid research (see Joyce Milton, *The Road to Malpsychia* [San Francisco: Encounter Books, 2002], esp. chap. 1; and E. Michael Jones, *Degenerate Moderns* [San Francisco: Ignatius Press, 1993], esp. pp. 19–41).

9. It is noteworthy that a similar conclusion was *not* drawn for other domains, say, in medicine or the theory of nature—though that too has been recently toyed with in academia in the name of diversity and "the Other."

10. Alfred I. Tauber, one of the most insightful writers in medical ethics today, has commented: "As long as the Self remains in doubt, ill defined by the epistemological quandary of modern analytic thought, we will be thwarted in our efforts to find a firm foundation for medical philosophy. . . . It seems to me that a crucial first step in articulating such a philosophy is to arrest the attack on the Self and to seek to salvage it as a vehicle for a moral philosophy" (*Confessions of a Medicine Man* [Boston: MIT Press, 1999], p. 85). The problem of the disappearing self in psychology was thoroughly canvassed many years ago by Carl Jung in his *Modern Man in Search of a Soul* (London: Paul, Trench, Trubner, 1933).

11. The awkward and forced identification of "good" and "happiness" with *pleasure* in the theory of hedonistic utilitarianism (Jeremy Bentham and John Stuart Mill) is either an arbitrary stipulation or a nest of confusions. This prevents the well-known slogan "The greatest happiness for the greatest number" from ever having any clear application in policy and life.

12. Diversity and tolerance are, of course, simply specific applications, and very important ones, of the Christian moral system. When uprooted from their Christian understanding as virtues of the heart, they degenerate into mere legal, external arrangements that fail to achieve the good upon which they are focused by nature.

13. On this point, see the carefully elaborated argument in Russ Shafer-Landau, *Whatever Happened to Good and Evil?* (New York: Oxford University Press, 2004).

14. Notoriously, people who *claim* to be loving have practiced great injustices, often posing as followers of Jesus Christ. But the prophetic tradition of the Bible and Jesus himself mercilessly excoriate such people.

15. Simon Blackburn, *Being Good: A Short Introduction to Ethics* (New York: Oxford University Press, 2001), pp. 132–33. What Confucius had in mind by "benevolence" is hardly what would come to mind with that word today. Richard Taylor claims: "The ultimate moral aspiration is simply this: *To be a warm-hearted and loving human being.* I call this an *ultimate* aspiration because no question of *why* can be asked concerning it, without misunderstanding it" (*Good and Evil* [New York: Macmillan, 1970], p. 255; chaps. 16–17 of this book contain a very helpful discussion of love). William Frankena briefly elaborates an ethic of love in his *Ethics,* 2d ed. (Englewood Cliffs, NJ: Prentice-Hall, 1963), chap. 3. A very thorough examination of love as an ethical concept is given in Gene Outka, *Agape: An Ethical Analysis* (New Haven, CT, and London: Yale University Press, 1972). In the field of New Testament studies, see Victor Paul Furnish, *The Love Command in the New Testament* (Nashville, TN: Abingdon, 1975).

16. Blackburn, *Being Good,* p. 134.

17. Hilary Putnam, *Ethics Without Ontology* (Cambridge, MA: Harvard University Press, 2004), p. 23.
18. Putnam, *Ethics Without Ontology*, p. 24.
19. He gave as *the* mark of his students that they have *agape* love *for one another* of the type he had exercised and exemplified toward them (John 13:34–35).
20. And some, not missing a beat, cook up a special ritual of "foot washing" that misses his whole point. "Washing feet" was only *one* way of serving those close by.
21. We recall the profound insights of Reinhold Niebuhr in *Moral Man and Immoral Society* (New York: Scribner, 1932) and the more widely known effects of "mob psychology" and "group think."
22. There is a veritable sea of literature on love. Here I have wanted to emphasize how love forces its way into the most arid stretches of ethical "theory" today, even where it and its Great Advocate cannot be *explicitly* embraced. To carry on the study, one might turn to Pitirim Sorokin, *The Ways and Power of Love* (Philadelphia: Templeton Foundation, 2002); Victor Paul Furnish, *The Love Command in the New Testament* (Nashville, TN: Abingdon Press, 1972); and, very recently, John Townsend, *Loving People* (Nashville, TN: Thomas Nelson, 2007). Art Lindsley's *Love: The Ultimate Apologetic* (Downers Grove, IL: InterVarsity, 2008) rightly emphasizes the indispensable role of love lived out in presenting Christ to the contemporary world.

CHAPTER 4: CAN WE KNOW THAT GOD EXISTS?

1. A description by an earlier writer, Adam Clarke, represents more fully the God of this tradition, though in mind-numbing phraseology. God is "the eternal, independent, and self-existent Being; the Being whose purposes and actions spring from himself, without foreign motive or influence; he who is absolute in dominion; the most pure, the most simple, the most spiritual of all essences; infinitely perfect; and eternally self-sufficient, needing nothing that he has made; illimitable in his immensity, inconceivable in his mode of existence, and indescribable in his essence; known fully only by himself, because an infinite mind can only be fully comprehended by itself. In a word, a Being who, from his infinite wisdom, cannot err or be deceived, and from his infinite goodness, can do nothing but what is eternally just, and right, and kind" (in John M'Clintock and James Strong, *Cyclopaedia*, vol. 3 [New York: Harper & Brothers, 1894], pp. 903–4).
2. Some of the most widely familiar biblical expressions of this view of God and his people are, of course, Psalm 23, the Lord's Prayer, and Romans 8.
3. Plato, *Laws*, bk. 10, Stephanus, pp. 887–98. This argument continues to be used up to Ralph Cudworth in the seventeenth century and even has its strong advocates today.

4. Epictetus, *Discourses*, bk. 1, chap. 16, "Of Providence." See *The Moral Discourses of Epictetus*, trans. Elizabeth Carter (London: Dent, 1910), p. 14.
5. David Hume, *The Natural History of Religion*, ed. H. E. Root (1757; London: Adam and Charles Black, 1956), "Author's Introduction," p. 21.
6. David Hume, *Dialogues Concerning Natural Religion*, ed. Richard H. Popkin (Indianapolis, IN: Hackett, 1982), next to last paragraph of pt. 12, p. 88. Since in contemporary thought many who reject the existence of God want Hume on their side, there is a constant battle over how the statements just quoted are to be taken. I will only point out here that, taken at face value, they are entirely consistent with Hume's account of rational belief formation. He does not claim we can *know* that God exists, just that it is rational to *believe* it and irrational not to.
7. Currently the most notorious case is Antony Flew. See his *There Is a God: How the World's Most Notorious Atheist Changed His Mind* (San Francisco: HarperOne, 2007). Along the same lines, see Francis S. Collins, *The Language of God* (New York: Free Press, 2006).
8. I recall watching the television journalist Garrick Utley reading the news of the discovery of the background radiation with wide-eyed astonishment, believing it to be confirmation of creation. He was justified in his response. It was the best news that ever came over NBC.
9. It is a view that has had a great deal of popular currency in our day, what with the "Age of Aquarius" and so forth. In Western thought Baruch Spinoza, Immanuel Kant, Arthur Schopenhauer, F. H. Bradley, and Martin Heidegger are among its practitioners.
10. These traditional reasons can be developed in numerous ways, all collectable under the heading of the "cosmological argument." There are, actually, cosmological arguments, in the plural. They are most famously associated with St. Thomas Aquinas, but in recent times with William Lane Craig. See Craig's *The Existence of God and the Beginning of the Universe* (San Bernardino, CA: Here's Life Publishers, 1979). Also see J. P. Moreland and William Lane Craig, *Philosophical Foundations for a Christian Worldview* (Downers Grove, IL: InterVarsity, 2003), chap. 23. (This book is a modern-day *Summa Contra Gentiles!*) For the usual "back and forth" of philosophers on these matters, see Donald R. Burrill, ed., *The Cosmological Arguments: A Spectrum of Opinion* (Garden City, NY: Doubleday Anchor, 1967). It is to be noted that the argument in this chapter does not concern the question "Why is there something rather than nothing?" Here it is simply a question of the existence of the physical universe.
11. For an accessible treatment of some of the more unlikely efforts to avoid the conclusion drawn here, I recommended W. David Beck, "God's Existence," in R. Douglas Geivett and Gary R. Habermas, eds., *In Defense of Miracles* (Downers Grove, IL: InterVarsity, 1997), pp. 149–62. Also see Moreland and Craig, *Philosophical Foundations for a Christian Worldview*.

12. By the editors of Time-Life Books, *Cosmos* (Alexandria, VA: Time-Life Books, 1989), p. 13.

CHAPTER 5: THE MIRACULOUS, AND CHRIST'S PRESENCE IN OUR WORLD

1. C. S. Lewis, *Mere Christianity* (New York: Macmillan, 1956), pp. 17–18. "Mere" Christianity is the central core of historic Christianity shorn of all the fringe elements that show up in this or that subgroup or denomination.

2. See Hume's *Dialogues Concerning Natural Religion,* pt. 12, for an example of a perfect tirade against the superstition and "enthusiasm" of those who claim to have "revelations" from God and how that perverts the "true" moral virtue in which God is supposedly interested.

3. David Hume, in *The Natural History of Religion,* purports to trace the rise of religion among humans to "a concern with regard to the events of life, and from the incessant hopes and fears, which actuate the human mind" (ed. H. E. Root [1757; London: Adam and Charles Black, 1956], p. 27). This led to polytheism, which he took to be the first form of religion, with its many gods who each deal with some particular human concern. Concocting "psychological origins" of religion becomes a preoccupation of thinkers from Hume well into the twentieth century.

4. James Orr, *The Problem of the Old Testament, Considered with Reference to Recent Criticism* (New York: Scribner, 1921), p. 10.

5. A major leader in advancing this view and establishing it as normative in the field of Old Testament studies was Abraham Kuenen (1828–91).

6. I realize, of course, that universities have also been called "secular" to indicate the absence of governance or financial support by ecclesiastical organizations. But that usage has almost totally disappeared as the idea of secular *knowledge* has emerged. What is now understood is that *secular* universities present knowledge as secular and that only secularized knowledge and research are practiced by them. Secular knowledge and research are those that have no essential reference to God except possibly negatively.

7. See C. S. Lewis, *Miracles,* chaps. 2, 8, many editions. In the Christian understanding of the Cosmic Christ, he is the one who made, sustains, and regulates the physical universe. See John 1:3; Col. 1:17; Heb. 1:2–3.

8. Norwood Russell Hanson, *What I Do Not Believe, and Other Essays,* ed. Stephen Toulmin and Harry Woolf (Dordrecht, Holland: Reidel, 1971), pp. 313–14. This is just the typical "village atheist" trick of a bygone era, as practiced, for example, by Robert Ingersoll and others. Ingersoll used to place his watch on the podium and invite God to strike him dead in fifteen minutes. Unsurprisingly, God never bothered.

9. For the full treatment, see "The Essay on Miracles," in David Hume, *Essays Moral, Political and Literary,* World's Classics Series (London:

Oxford University Press, 1963), pp. 517–44; see also *An Enquiry Concerning Human Understanding*, chap. 10.

10. On this remarkable transition in the world of the early Christians, see Rodney Stark's *Cities of God* (San Francisco: HarperSanFrancisco, 2006). According to Stark, within three hundred years of the death of Christ, 50 percent of the population of the cities in the Roman Empire were Christian. More important, see his account of the role moral transformation of individuals played in this social transformation. For a much earlier account of this transformation, see William Paley, *A View of the Evidences of Christianity* (1794); also as *The Works of William Paley*, vol. 4 (London: Thomas Tegg, 1825).

11. On this see N. T. Wright's recent book, *Surprised by Hope: Rethinking Heaven, the Resurrection, and the Mission of the Church* (San Francisco: HarperOne, 2008).

12. Wolfhart Pannenberg, *The Historicity of Nature: Essays on Science and Theology* (West Conshohocken, PA: Templeton Foundation, 2008), pp. 210–11. On Tipler's discussion, see Frank Tipler, *The Physics of Immortality* (New York: Doubleday, 1994).

13. See William Paley, *A View of the Evidences of Christianity*, many editions; and William Lane Craig's many publications on Christ's resurrection. See also Frank Morison, *Who Moved the Stone?* (Grand Rapids, MI: Zondervan, 1987. First edition, 1930.)

14. N. T. Wright, "How Do We Know That Jesus Existed?" in Antony Flew, *There Is a God* (San Francisco: HarperOne, 2007), Appendix B, pp. 112–13. For Wright's extensive discussions of Christ's resurrection, its nature, and its actuality, see his *Surprised by Hope*.

15. Roger Martin, *R. A. Torrey: Apostle of Certainty* (Murfreesboro, TN: Sword of the Lord Publishers, 1976), pp. 76–81.

CHAPTER 6: KNOWLEDGE OF CHRIST IN THE SPIRITUAL LIFE

1. Gotthold Lessing, *Lessing's Theological Writings*, trans. Henry Chadwick (Stanford, CA: Stanford University Press, 1967), p. 55.

2. Peter L. Berger, *The Precarious Vision* (Garden City, NY: Doubleday, 1961), p. 7.

3. Berger, *Precarious Vision*, p. 21.

4. Berger, *Precarious Vision*, p. 22.

5. Berger, *Precarious Vision*, p. 163.

6. Berger, *Precarious Vision*, p. 162.

7. Wilhelm Herrmann, *The Communion of the Christian with God*, 3rd Eng. ed., trans. J. Sandys Stanyon (New York: Putnam, 1909), p. 92.

8. A. N. Wilson, *How Can We Know? An Essay on the Christian Religion* (New York: Atheneum, 1985), p. x.

9. Frank Laubach, *Letters by a Modern Mystic* (Syracuse, NY: New Readers Press, 1955), and numerous other editions including *Letters by a Modern Mystic* (Colorado Springs, CO: Purposeful Design Publications, 2007). See also Frank C. Laubach, *Man of Prayer: Selected Writings of a World Missionary* (Syracuse, NY: Laubach Literacy International, 1990) for this and other of his writings.

10. Laubach, *Letters by a Modern Mystic*, p. 15.

11. Laubach, *Letters by a Modern Mystic*, p. 16. Multitudes of people have entered into the kingdom life of which Laubach speaks. Names such as E. Stanley Jones and Agnes Sanford come to mind among more recent teachers and writers concerning it. But see the rich array of practitioners discussed in Richard Foster, *Streams of Living Water* (San Francisco: HarperSanFrancisco, 1998), and in J. Gilchrist Lawson, *Deeper Experiences of Famous Christians* (New Kensington, PA: Whitaker House, 1998). On the "with God" life, see the very instructive introductory sections of *The Renovaré Spiritual Formation Bible* (San Francisco: HarperSanFrancisco, 2005). The spiritual life as reflected in literature of the Christian ages is an inexhaustible resource for deepening what we are talking about in this chapter. Those who wish to inform themselves about the nature and reality of the spiritual life in Christ have only to acquaint themselves with what actually happens in the lives of his people. See Patrick Sherry, *Spirit, Saints and Immortality* (Albany: State University of New York Press, 1984).

12. Among the very greatest of these are Thomas à Kempis, William Law, Richard Baxter, Jeremy Taylor, and Francis de Sales. For a quick but effective introduction to others, see Lawson, *Deeper Experiences of Famous Christians*.

13. Laubach, *Man of Prayer*, p. 154.

14. See Richard Foster, *Celebration of Discipline* (San Francisco: Harper & Row, 1988) and Dallas Willard, *The Spirit of the Disciplines* (San Francisco: Harper & Row, 1988) for a fuller treatment of spiritual disciplines.

15. Your "kingdom"—and you certainly have one, provided by God—is the range of your effective will. It is what you have "say" over.

16. I have tried to be helpful with this subtle but profoundly important aspect of spiritual life in Christ in my book *Hearing God: Developing a Conversational Relationship with God* (Downers Grove, IL: InterVarsity, 1999), first published as *In Search of Guidance* (1984).

17. See William James, *The Varieties of Religious Experience,* "Conclusions" (Lecture 20), many editions.

CHAPTER 7: KNOWLEDGE OF CHRIST AND CHRISTIAN PLURALISM

1. Of course, my *views* on any subject, including religion, might be better than some others—more true, let us say—without my being a *better person* than people who hold other views. But that is often overlooked.

2. In any group, the vast majority of those in "good standing" do *not* believe many of the things the leaders of the group teach as "necessary." More often than not they don't even know about them, and if they did, they would not be able to understand them. An example of this would be what is stated about salvation in the Athanasian Creed. After laying out extremely subtle points about the Trinity, it is declared there that "he therefore that will be saved must think thus of the Trinity, . . . neither confounding the Persons, nor dividing the Substance" of the Trinity. The issues in this creed are extremely important. But if one must "think thus" to be saved, 99 percent of professing Christians are not going to make it. Try this creed on and see what you think. Groups and their institutions tend to confuse *what they need to teach* with *what one must believe in order to be saved*. This leads to their members *professing* lots of things they neither believe nor are committed to—indeed, do not even understand. That, in turn, makes it inevitable that they will not "live up to what they profess," for they actually do not believe what they profess. The effects of this on genuinely trusting and following Christ are *devastating*. They can be abundantly observed in most Christian groups.

3. Sometimes the question is asked, "Is there only one true religion or are there many?" Schubert M. Ogden has written a helpful book by that very title (Dallas, TX: Southern Methodist University Press, 1992). But this way of putting the question seems to take religions as social-historical wholes, and it would be hard to sustain the view that everything involved in any religion as a concrete reality is true. There is much more to Christianity as a historical reality than the Apostles' Creed or "mere Christianity," which we are focusing upon here. And the history of Christianity itself gives rise to the painful question, "Is there only one true 'denomination' or form of *Christianity* or are there many?" How would one answer that? We know how it has been answered in the bitter and brutal past of Christianity itself..

4. In particular we have to ask, "Does strong pluralism exist only on the assumption that religion is outside the domain of responsible belief or knowledge?" And, "Does the person who says that the differences between religions make no difference to God know enough about God to know that?"

5. Peter Berger, *The Precarious Vision* (Garden City, NY: Doubleday, 1961), p. 163. An obscure perception of this fact is what leads multitudes in Western societies today to say that they are very spiritual but not religious. They are operating from what has filtered down to them through their culture from Jesus. Where they go from there, however, is usually disastrous for lack of knowledge of Christ.

6. The situation is drastically worsened when one realizes that particular groups have in mind *their particular version* of the historical personage.

Thus "exclusiveness" is applied not just to "Christianity" with respect to other religions, but also to particular versions of Christianity. This was very common fifty years ago and still persists in some quarters. In living memory, some Christian denominations explicitly rejected the possibility of members of other denominations "making it in." By contrast, anyone who concedes that children who die without information about the historical Jesus will not be rejected by God has accepted the essential point of Christian pluralism. They "come to God" without knowledge of Jesus.

7. *Newsweek,* August 14, 2006, p. 43. When we speak of a good Christian, Jew, Muslim, and so forth, the emphasis may fall in one of two places: a *good* Christian or a good *Christian.* It makes all the difference in the world, since a "good" Christian, Jew, or Muslim need not be a good person, one pleasing and acceptable to God. Often he or she is not.

CHAPTER 8: PASTORS AS TEACHERS OF THE NATIONS

1. See the study by Pitirim Sorokin, *The Crisis of Our Age* (New York: Dutton, 1941). Our profoundly addictive society is founded upon our worship of feelings.

2. This is one major dimension of the massive and thoughtless "flight from God" that took place in the second quarter of the last century. See Max Picard, *The Flight from God,* trans. J. M. Cameron (Chicago: Regnery, 1951).

3. John Oman, *Grace and Personality,* 4th ed. (Cambridge: Cambridge University Press, 1931), p. 143.

4. See George Marsden, *The Soul of the American University: From Protestant Establishment to Established Nonbelief* (New York: Oxford University Press, 1994).

5. Mark Noll opens chapter 1 of his *The Scandal of the Evangelical Mind* (Grand Rapids, MI: Eerdmans, 1994) with the sentence: "The scandal of the evangelical mind is that there is not much of an evangelical mind" (p. 3). But the root of that "scandal," if it is one, is that evangelical religion defines its content with no reference to knowledge. In fact, as things now stand and have stood for decades, Christianity as a whole has no essential tie to knowledge. We looked briefly at the history of this in Chapter 1. It is not clear why anyone who understands the situation would find a scandal here. What exactly is it that is thought to be worthy of reproach? By whom? Why?

6. See William Heatley's excellent book *The Gift of Work* (Colorado Springs, CO: NavPress, 2008).

7. Paula Houston, "Salvation Workout," *Christian Century,* April 8, 2008, p. 35.

Acknowledgments

I AM GRATEFUL for the help of Jan Johnson, Keith Matthews, Becky Heatley, Bill Heatley, Jere Underwood, K. Bruce Miller, and Greg Jesson in the development of this book. The book was occasioned by a series of eight talks on the theme "Knowledge of Christ in Today's World." The talks were audiotaped at the home of Mr. and Mrs. Paul Wolfe and produced for distribution by Thomas Dervartanian with the Eidos Christian Center (eidos@earthlink.net). Jan Johnson transcribed the entire audio series to provide a text that substantially corresponds to the text of this book. I am very grateful for the patient encouragement and guidance of Michael Maudlin at HarperOne, and for the assistance of Lisa Zuniga, who made this a much better book than it otherwise would have been.

Subject Index

Scripture Index